Key West

COTTAGES AND GARDENS

Entrance to "Elegant Retreat For One."

Key West

COTTAGES AND GARDENS

Inspiration from America's Special Topical Island

Leslie Linsley

Pineapple Press
Palm Beach, Florida

Pineapple Press
An imprint of Globe Pequot, the trade division of
The Rowman & Littlefield Publishing Group, Inc.
4501 Forbes Blvd., Ste. 200
Lanham, MD 20706
www.rowman.com

Distributed by NATIONAL BOOK NETWORK

British Library Cataloguing in Publication Information available

Library of Congress Cataloging-in-Publication Data

Names: Linsley, Leslie, author.
Title: Key West cottages and gardens : inspiration from an American
   tropical island / Leslie Linsley.
Description: Palm Beach, Florida : Pineapple Press, [2023]
Identifiers: LCCN 2022042314 (print) | LCCN 2022042315 (ebook) | ISBN
   9781683343370 (cloth) | ISBN 9781683343387 (epub)
Subjects: LCSH: Cottages--Florida--Key West--Decoration. | Interior
   decoration--Florida--Key West. | Cottage gardens--Florida--Key West.
Classification: LCC NK2195.C67 L55 2023 (print) | LCC NK2195.C67 (ebook)
   | DDC 747/.88370975941--dc23/eng/20221021
LC record available at https://lccn.loc.gov/2022042314
LC ebook record available at https://lccn.loc.gov/2022042315

∞™ The paper used in this publication meets the minimum requirements of
American National Standard for Information Sciences—Permanence of Paper
for Printed Library Materials, ANSI/NISO Z39.48-1992.

Printed in China

This book is dedicated to Jon Aron, my late husband,
book partner, and best friend for 42 years.

Sign at Key West International Airport.

Contents

A sculpture of Marilyn Monroe in her famous pose in front of the Tropic Cinema.

Welcome to Key West

"Forty-two degrees in Dallas, six degrees in Boston, snowing from Maine to Washington. The only warm place in the entire country on this February day is Key West, Florida, where the temperature is eighty-two. Even Miami is experiencing an unusual cold spell of fifty-five degrees." This weather report simply confirms what most inhabitants of the southernmost tip of the continental United States already know: Key West is a tropical paradise.

Many years ago, my husband and partner, Jon Aron, and I produced a coffee table–style book, *Nantucket Island Living.* It had just been released when we received a message from our editor: "How would you guys like to do a book on Key West houses this winter?" The timing was perfect. Since we lived on Nantucket Island, off the coast of Massachusetts, where the winter can be rather bleak, the prospect of having such a plum job plunked into our laps was heavenly. Jon was a photographer and art director and we had collaborated on over forty books together. We had never been to Key West, but we had many friends who owned houses, or spent part of the winter there and had suggested that we would love this southernmost island. They vehemently boasted, "It's not like any other place in the state of Florida."

We rented a house for two months and left to spend February and March in the southernmost city in the United States. Little did we know how little we didn't know. Jon had been used to photographing with the diffused lighting of Nantucket and was totally unprepared for the extremely bright light in Key West. When I wasn't contacting homeowners to shoot their homes, I was in the library doing research. At that time, Key West was pretty rustic, if not downright shabby. The homeowners whose houses we included in that first book became friends. Over the years many moved to other homes that we photographed for magazine articles and then produced another book, *Key West: A Tropical Lifestyle*, in 2007. We returned every winter since that first book was published, making friends, and becoming part of this community. I began writing a weekly newspaper column, "At Home in Key West," for the *Key West Citizen*. And then, two years ago, during the pandemic, while working on a book about grief (Jon had died the year before), I realized it was time for a new book about the cottages of Key West. The style of the houses and the lifestyle of its residents were changing. Gentrification, here as elsewhere, was creeping into Key West, and this funky little out-of-the-way place, was being discovered by a new crop of potential homeowners.

As more people began working from home, it was no longer necessary to commute to an office. People began to realize they could choose desirable places anywhere in the country from which to work. With its consistently good weather, real estate in Key West soared in value. The little Conch cottages were being bought up, remodeled, and were contributing to the gentrification of the island. I wanted to find the best of these

renovations, done with taste and respect for what Key West has held most valuable: individuality, its history, its culture, its creativity, and most of all a sense of being connected to the community. And although gentrification of Key West is celebrated by some and opposed by others, the fact remains that people who have the means to go anywhere in the world keep coming back to this place. Key West grows on you. It just feels good to be here.

While Key West is changing, many of the locals long for the old days when they could belly up to the bar at Sloppy Joe's or the Green Parrott and talk about the famous writers like Ernest Hemingway or Tennessee Williams who held forth, on those same stools, with a good yarn. They mourn the changes. But a vast number of like-minded people appreciate a place with history, a place where the community is committed to preserving a laid-back lifestyle, where artists and millionaires live side by side and you can't tell the difference, and everyone appreciates the natural beauty and has a healthy respect for the environment.

Each time we returned we would ask ourselves, "What is it that intrigues us so about this little spit of land located 150 miles south of Miami and ninety miles north of Cuba?" For one thing, it is the only subtropical city in the continental United States, which means the weather is consistently beautiful year-round. For another, it is an island that is connected to the mainland, but only barely, by a two-lane highway to Miami, with water on both sides of the road. It is only four miles long and one mile wide and, for the most part, is surrounded by a coral reef. This sets it apart from the rest of Florida and pretty much guarantees the small-town community atmosphere that has always prevailed, even with its

The Studios and Books and Books is a Key West magnet on the corner of Simonton and Eaton Streets.

Harpoon Harry's diner on Caroline Street.

year-round population of 35,000 permanent residents. During the season, Key West plays host to over two million visitors from around the world, many coming in on cruise ships that, until the pandemic, docked routinely at Mallory Square. While most residents find this a negative aspect of daily living, others feel the positive impact of the revenue they generate. Control over size and number of ships in port has caused an ongoing political battle as they begin to return.

There is the Tropic Cinema, a first-run, state-of-the-art movie theater, the Studios of Key West offering exhibits and art classes, Books and Books, a top-notch independent bookstore, the Key West Symphony, many live performances at local theaters, music of all venues, over two hundred restaurants, a variety of historic buildings offering exciting exhibits and social events, the Monroe County Library that hosts author presentations, and an overwhelming number of outdoor activities—in the dead of winter!

It is an island where the preferred mode of transportation is still the bicycle; everything is within walking distance, unlike the rest of Florida with its superhighways. And while gentrification is on the move, it is happening here at a typical Key West pace.

For several months last year, I had the privilege of being in many homes around town. They are owned by people who saw and felt something in this community that made them want to belong. Some of the homeowners have been here for a lifetime, some are newly arrived, some are from other countries, and many from every state in the Union. The variety of homeowners on this island is as varied as it has always been, coming here from all walks of life and contributing to the island image of being an offbeat, laid back,

interesting place. Key West is the perfect vacation place for many, and the final destination for others. But what is obvious about the community is that Key West is ruled by tolerance, kindness, devotion to community, and a respect for idiosyncrasy. A quirkiness prevails. The residents are independent, offbeat, and have been drawn here by the weather first and foremost, as well as a lifestyle that has attracted free spirits since its inception. While there are beautiful mansions on the waterfront, and large estates throughout the island, the prevailing structures are small shotgun houses and wood-frame cottages once built to house the cigarmakers who came from Cuba to work in the cigar factories. These structures are called Conch cottages (pronounced "kongk"), which means all things local, and make up the overwhelming charm of Old Town. Key West has become a small town with a sophisticated mentality. It overflows with cultural events featuring internationally known figures. Through all its changes, Key West has never lost its fundamental joie de vivre.

While working on this book, I've not only found incredibly interesting homes, but also homeowners who are committed to being part of this community. And their homes reflect a sense of style and good taste, infused with local paintings and crafts, collections from world travels, local sources, and salvaged materials from historic buildings. All the homes are designed for easy indoor/outdoor living that reflects a tropical lifestyle. Some incorporate the newest gadgets, unpretentious, offhandedly chic furnishings, and fascinating approaches to designing gardens. Others reflect a desire to preserve the past with respect for its history. Owning a home in Key West is a privilege and the homes included here are just a small example of the breadth of creativity found throughout Key West.

Gentrification, in many desirable places, often manifests itself by whitewashing the things inherent to a building's history and location. I was fearful that Key West was in danger of losing its edginess, as homes are being renovated, and sometimes stripped of their interior uniqueness and artistic attitude. An example in Key West is found in the early houses that were built with Dade County pine walls. When respected and left untouched, this type of pine wall is a source of pride, often pointed out by homeowners to visitors who are new to the island. With the restrictions of land size and height, the small Conch cottages are limited to what can be done within the original footprint. This is an interesting challenge. With limitations come creative solutions, or a way to embrace rather than disguise space. A place should dictate how it can best be designed with respect to its original intent, while incorporating modern amenities for the lifestyle and aesthetic of its owner or owners.

In every home we photographed, highlighting aspects of importance, such as high ceilings, molding details, original wood or Cuban-tiled floors, and the incorporation of indoor/outdoor living, the homeowners have demonstrated original and responsible approaches to restoration, renovation, decoration, and repurposing. For the most part, the homes offer some of the best examples of living large in small spaces.

Key West home style is reflected in a sense of spontaneity, unfettered experimentation, and a nod to its historic roots. The interest often comes from unexpected pairings of seemingly unrelated objects or material. For example, an industrial-style lamp might be paired with a chair upholstered in eggplant velvet, a sleek new kitchen displays a flashing commercial sign reclaimed from an industrial building, the old and the new, the chic and the funky, an Hermes orange throw over a curbside-found chair. It was reassuring to find all this and more reassurances that Key West has not lost its offbeat and confident attitude. Key West style is simply being redefined for how we live now and what is possible.

I've produced more than forty coffee table–style books and the process is always exciting. What could be better than making a living as a house voyeur? As a journalist I love nothing more than interviewing people about their homes, why they did what they did, what they love most about their houses and their community. Pride of home is exciting to reveal.

I was quite overwhelmed with the generosity of homeowners, many unknown to me before, who enthusiastically opened their homes to our invasion. Hopefully we have been respectful of the opportunity. These houses represent a microcosm of homes that make up the current community of the core district of Key West, and this book introduces homeowners who are contributing to the future of the island.

These island homes are owned by artists, architects, product designers, an interior designer, real estate agents, doctors, businesspeople, innkeepers, a gallery owner, preservationists, a therapist, a literary agent, singles, longtime mates, writers, and retirees. Most are civic minded and involved with community, preservation of the island, and political and cultural affairs. Many volunteer their time for worthy causes and activities of interest.

The focus of this book is an intimate peek into the small cottages that contribute to the visual

Harpoon Harry's, an iconic diner.

A sand sculpture at the beach at Casa Marina Hotel.

charm of Key West. As the community is changing, so are the interiors of many of the old houses. With understanding and respect, their history is not being destroyed. For the most part the changes seem to be an exciting redefinition of the current Key West style that seamlessly melds the old with the new. One house is filled with authentic Key West memorabilia; another incorporated salvaged shutters from a famous author's home. A year-round homeowner furnished her home with artifacts from years of traveling around the world. One couple, product designers, joined two small cottages and modernized the interior with an exquisite approach to minimalism. A single man lives in three rooms, meticulously planned to showcase his collections of retro items. It is a true nod to old Key West. The showcased homes reveal a variety of interior designs with unique furnishings, colors, materials, accessories, and artwork, and, for the most part, in homes that are less than 1,000 square feet. Their approaches to decorating are inspirational for homeowners, no matter where they live.

The Birth of a Book

A collaboration of creative people will create an environment where they feed off one another. Different aspects of the creative process, and each person's experience, coalesce to bring out the best results. When the right talent comes together, the outcome is most satisfying for all who have participated, including, ultimately, the reader.

Michael Pelkey, my longtime friend and decorator of dozens of Key West homes, has styled the rooms, enlivening them with artful arrangements of fruits and vegetables, flowers and table settings, and interesting additions to complement the architecture and home furnishings in each of the rooms. His solutions to furnishing any space are at once inventive and sophisticated, yet at the same time comfortable and intimate. He has a knack for putting the right elements together and has total confidence in what works. He knows how to inject a sense of energy into a lovely, but static space, and is never afraid to experiment. He knows instinctively exactly what a room needs to make it come alive. Michael's own home has been featured in dozens of magazine articles and several books, as well as on the cover of my last Key West book. For many years, Michael was a private chef to a renowned Key West resident, and his visual presentations are as noted as the food he prepares, dissolving boundaries between disciplines. He has created the excitement of activity in each home, revealing how a room might be used, indicating that people live here and share their homes with friends.

Tamara Alvarez has much experience photographing island homes and the magnificent gardens and tropical plantings around the island. Her work has appeared in many national magazines, most notably on the covers of *Ocean Home* and *Florida Design Miami*. She has a BA in visual arts from Emily Carr University of Art and Design. Her photographs of the homes showcased here express an intimacy that will draw you into the lifestyle of the homeowners. I hope you will experience what we experienced while working on this book.

A Brief History of Florida's Southernmost Island

Key West's history begins like many small towns in this country. Unlike a true island, surrounded by water, Key West can be reached by car, via its two-lane highway from the mainland. Key West has endured many industry collapses during its two-century history. But its residents have always been a resilient bunch and proven to have the ability to reinvent themselves and always find the next successful business opportunity.

Key West grew during its history through development and changes in migration patterns, advances in transportation and commerce, and historical milestones like the Civil War, the Great Depression, and World War II. Key West boasts a colorful history. In 1815 King Ferdinand VII of Spain gave the island to infantryman Juan Pablo Salas as a reward for unspecified services. While living in Havana, Cuba, in 1821 Salas met American financier John Simonton in a bar and sold the property to him for two thousand dollars. As a savvy businessman, Simonton sold off parts of the island to fellow businessmen John Fleming, John Whitehead, and Pardon Greene, all of whom became prominent citizens of Key West. Streets in Old Town bear their names.

Key West was an ideal location for an international port. Though surrounded by coral reefs, ships could travel easily through four channels leading to its natural harbor. Simonton was aware of the island's strategic position and, through his connections in Washington, he was able to establish Key West as an American port of entry, guaranteed to build an economy.

In 1822, when Florida was ceded to the United States, the federal government took possession of Key West. Four years later, a naval base was established on the island in order to rid the surrounding waters of the piracy that was threatening the growing economy of the island. For the next 150 years a major portion of the island's land area was devoted to United States Navy operations.

In 1828 the settlement at Key West was incorporated as a city. The first houses were built in a cluster on the northwestern tip of the island. By 1831, there were eighty-one residential and commercial buildings in Key West. The population hovered at 360.

During the nineteenth century, sea traffic, making its way from Havana through the treacherous, reef-filled waters surrounding Key West created a "wrecker's paradise." Many of the island's early settlers, who had been New England seafarers, saw the financial possibilities in salvaging cargo from ships wrecked on the coral reefs. There were plenty of shipwrecks to support the island's population in salvage business and many of the grandest island houses were built with the wood salvaged from the wrecked ships and furnished with the fine cargo found on board.

To organize the wrecking industry, the United States government established a court on the island to determine the value of the salvaged cargo. Washington passed a law requiring all ships wrecked in American waters be brought to the nearest American port. As a result the wrecking business in the British colony of the Bahamas dropped considerably and many ambitious Bahamians moved to Key West to pursue their livelihood—becoming American citizens. By 1855 wrecking was a big business on the island. During that time, however, several lighthouses were built to mark the reefs, greatly reducing the number of shipwrecks off Key West and the wrecking business slowly died out.

At the same time sponging and turtling were also thriving businesses until the 1960s when the sea turtle was declared an endangered species and turtling was outlawed in the United States. The development of the sponging industry attracted

Bahamian wreckers and fishermen who settled in Key West and by 1892, 8,000 of the 25,000 Key West residents were of Bahamian origin.

Three years after the end of the American Civil War, Spanish dominance of Cuba ignited a revolutionary struggle that started a ten-year war. Many Cubans fled their country for Key West, the nearest friendly port. They brought with them the industry of manufacturing handmade cigars. By the late nineteenth century there were 166 cigar factories in Key West employing thousands of workers. The growth of the cigarmaking business increased revenue in the city and by 1880 Key West was not only the wealthiest city per capita in the United States, but also the largest city in Florida. Also, since it could not be reached by land, it attracted more American ships than all other United States ports combined.

As you can imagine, all this activity and affluence brought about an overwhelming demand for housing. Those who came from all corners of the world introduced a wide variety of building styles. As a result of this variety of architecture and common use of wood as a building material, the buildings in Key West are distinct from those in other Florida cities.

Wood was readily available in Key West and the primary material employed in the construction of houses. Very few houses were built with plaster, which could crack if the building shifted in high winds or hurricanes. The interiors were also built of wood. Dade County pine strips were often placed horizontally to form paneled walls, in a way similar to the means of finishing the interior of a boat. The island's Historic District includes 3,000 wooden structures listed on the National Register of Historic Places.

Most of the early houses were built without the aid of an architect and, more often than not, designed as construction progressed. Those who had been ship's carpenters incorporated such practical conveniences as roof hatches for ventilation. Sea captains from New England often built sturdier, well-proportioned homes. Widow's walks, popular in coastal towns in New England, are seen atop the grander Key West houses lining the waterfront.

Along with the growth of residential construction, the commercial district of Key West also experienced a construction boom, slowed only in 1886 when an uncontrollable fire destroyed the entire wooden commercial district. Wharfs, warehouses, factories, stores, and City Hall were destroyed. However, business was hardly affected: sponging, cigarmaking, salvage and wrecking, fishing and retail operations continued to thrive and the commercial district was quickly rebuilt.

In 1890 the Naval Commandant's Quarters, popularly known as "The Little White House," was built on the local navy base. Intended for use by visiting presidents, only President Harry S. Truman actually stayed overnight in the building and returned ten times. The Little White House is now a museum in the Truman Annex complex.

In 1904 retired oil baron Henry Flagler, well known for his development of the resort city of Palm Beach, announced plans to build a railroad from Miami to Cuba. By 1912 Flagler's Overseas Railroad reached its last American stop, Key West. The connection to Cuba was never realized. With this overland connection, the population of Key West grew to 23,000 and an influx of fun-loving tourists discovered the island. Soon the small sponging boats were carrying bootleg whiskey to Key West from Havana. The roaring twenties were a high time on the island, ending with the advent of the Great Depression of the 1930s. The cigarmaking business began to dwindle, tourists stopped coming, and the railroad approached bankruptcy. In 1935 a hurricane destroyed so much of the railroad that for three years the island was cut off from the mainland once again. Federal funds were used to convert the railroad bridges to a two-lane highway. The car and truck connection revived the island's economy, making the island accessible to postwar American tourists.

In the later 1940s, the jumbo Gulf shrimp, known locally as "pink gold," became an industry that has survived to this day. With the increase in tourism, sportfishing became one of Key West's greatest attractions. The Gulf waters are filled with barracuda, sailfish, marlin, yellow and blackfin tuna, dolphin, bonefish, grouper, snapper, and mackerel.

Artists and writers have always been attracted to the "end of the line." Rich with natural beauty, Key West is one of the most romantic spots in the country. Its famous residents, Ernest Hemmingway and Tennessee Williams, attracted many people to the island and their presence is still felt throughout the city today. The fluctuations from natural and human disasters and the island's remoteness have been its best protection against modern building developments that could have destroyed its architectural character.

After 1974, when the navy closed some of its bases in Key West, the city focused on tourism. In the process of attracting more tourists, the island's residents and businesspeople concentrated on sprucing up. Gay people have always appreciated Key West's unique open atmosphere, and in the mid 1970s the city experienced an

Boating and water sports are popular all year long.

influx of businesses owned by members of the gay community. This, as well as organized gay cruises, have contributed to the island's economy and an atmosphere of acceptance of all different lifestyles by those who live or visit here.

Key West is exciting, eccentric, and eclectic. Even its most serious residents take time to join the crowds at the old Mallory Square dock at day's end to celebrate sunset with a round of applause. And while Key West is always changing, its residents are doing their best to keep the pace slow and to honor a community spirit.

In 1982 Key West was registered as a National Historic District, which helped with the preservation of Old Town. Guidelines for preservation, made available by the Historic Architectural Review Commission, and the Historic Florida Keys Foundation, as well as the annual Old Island Days House and Garden Tours, help promote an appreciation of Key West architecture.

Today, Key West is going through growing pains. Affordable housing, traffic overload, and lack of parking in town are just a few challenging problems for locals and visitors alike. Key West's history reveals, however, that the city has always reinvented itself and islanders recognize that growth is inevitable. But the island is already built up, and any remaining lots are small, limiting further expansion and almost guaranteeing that the more charming aspect of the island will remain intact.

What makes Key West so special? I kept asking the homeowners of the houses presented here, as well as friends and acquaintances new and old. Everyone says they come here for the weather. The island's tropical breezes keep the humidity lower than elsewhere in Florida and it's usually warmer than Miami. Then they quickly answer, "the people." Key West is accepting. Who you are, where you come from, or what you did or did not do in another life somewhere else does not matter. If you are here, you are accepted. It is a community where there is no ageism, and it is common to find people of all ages socializing with one another. People here are generous of their time and money, whether in the cause of mentoring a child or the preservation of historic buildings.

Key West's architecture is a charming, intriguing mélange of styles. They illustrate the creative and sensitive way people have designed their homes to suit this lifestyle. Together they offer inspirational ideas for renovation and interior design, as well as capturing an attitude for living. Every street and lane is rich with architectural variations and contradictions. The variety of building styles throughout Key West is a result of the blending of cultures, ideas, and construction techniques. The architectural details that were popular during the nineteenth century in other parts of the United States were applied in one way or another to houses in Key West.

Whether the stylistic influence is Classic Revival, West Indian, Folk, Victorian, or Queen Anne, the Key West version is generally smaller, simpler, and less ornate than comparable houses built in other regions.

The introduction of the scroll saw and turning lathe in the nineteenth century inspired a diversity of decorative architectural millwork. The resulting gingerbread trim can be seen on houses all over Old Town and lends a Victorian air to even the humblest cottages. While this type of trim was often mass-produced, many carpenters created their own designs, some announcing the profession of the homeowners, for example, gingerbread cutouts on a baker's home.

Small Houses

During the last quarter of the nineteenth century, a growing population of cigar-factory workers were brought to Key West. Most of the small houses were built to accommodate them. Often erected quickly, these simple houses, known as shotguns, face onto the street in order to maximize the number of house lots on a block, with a facade pierced only by a single door and window. These one-and-a-half-story houses were typically made of wood, without any decorative detail. The original dwellings were composed of three narrow rooms in a row, leading back from the front of the building. The front, rear, and interior doors were aligned, the idea being that one could fire a shot from the open front door clear through the house and out the back door.

Over the decades these houses have been renovated, removing walls to create a larger feeling, but due to the tightness of the land footprint, there are no expansion opportunities. A mini jungle of tropical plants and trees often creates a natural wall around property, providing complete privacy in Old Town, where the houses are built close together.

While many of these cottages have been purchased and remodeled by newcomers over the years, many remain in the hands of native Conch families. They are scattered throughout Old Town, often right at home on a street that boasts grand Victorian and Bahamian houses. This book concentrates on exposing the small cottages and overwhelmingly spectacular gardens that primarily represent the prevailing character of Old Town and its inhabitants today.

Key West is not like anywhere else in Florida and some residents and visitors alike think it should be its own state. It is certainly a state of mind. When you're in Key West you have the luxury of time. Living in Key West isn't for everyone, but for those who call this island home, the place, the people just spoke to them.

Chickens and roosters rule the roost in Key West.

Old Town

In 1982, the Old Town section of Key West was registered as a National Historic District. This area is comprised of more than 3,000 historic wood frame structures. Together these modest little homes impart a charm that evokes a timeless island past.

A mélange of different architectural styles sit side by side, some elaborate Victorians with gingerbread trim, built at the end of the nineteenth century, ornate Queen Anne cottages, Louisiana Creole cottages, and Key West tropical style. Every street and lane is rich with architectural variations and contradictions.

The Old Town cemetery is an interesting place to wander.

"BILLY" ON WILLIAM STREET

Laura Barletta has an exceptional eye for finding potential fixer-uppers and turning ugly ducklings into swans. Her company, Beautiful Interiors, has designed, renovated, and decorated dozens of houses for clients all over Key West. Often partnering with decorator Michael Pelkey, she is an expert at sourcing and repurposing vintage objects and is adept at infusing a room with pieces of diverse provenance, as well as flea market finds that are no less chic. She will go to any lengths to find just the right objects to inject character into a room.

As a lifelong art collector, she has a sixth sense about spotting the diamonds in the rough, as seen here in this warm and inviting cottage she renovated, expanded, and decorated. It is both sleek and imbued with Old World charm derived from an eclectic collection of art and artifacts. Laura's restoration and decoration of "Billy" (she names all the houses she works on) shows a confidence needed to infuse a home with surprises at every turn. Laura never does the expected. She has an innate ability to find exactly what a room needs and isn't afraid of experimentation. Beautiful Interiors exemplifies the art of surprise as evidenced in the large, black granite sinks she found in a nunnery in France and shipped home to use in the cottage kitchen.

The town of Key West lists this little Conch cottage as having been built in 1887 and originally owned by Thomas Rosco Roberts, a local electrician. Laura renovated this classical revival house in 2009. It had been used primarily as a rental property and was on a prime Old Town street. Notably, the famous American writer, poet, cartoonist, songwriter, playwright, and children's book author (*Where the Sidewalk Ends*, among many others) Shel Silverstein lived just two doors from this house, adding his illustrious presence to the neighborhood. The cottage had been previously owned by Don and Will (see their house, "Comfortable on Ashe Street" page 37), who did some renovations before moving on. These Old Town homes are often connected by owners who keep buying in the neighborhood and ultimately becoming friends.

This cottage and the large house on the corner of Southard are now one property, which allowed for a sizeable pool, and the creation of a mini family compound. The cottage is used for guests and family overflow when everyone gets together.

The cottage is set back from the sidewalk, separated by a neat, white picket fence. An inviting wide porch spans the facade. This small separation between the house and the public thoroughfare is unusual in Old Town. This type of one-and-a-half story structure is considered a classic revival, three bay with its roof ridge running parallel to the street. Laura completely reconfigured and doubled the size of the structure by adding a great room to the back that

A classic revival cottage in Old Town, this house has been responsibly restored and decorated with taste and style. The materials, furnishings, art, and artifacts were sourced from around the world by Beautiful Interiors.

The entire back wall of this great room opens to access the enclosed patio and pool. The refurbished warm wooden walls and ceiling, made of Dade County pine (some from the original structure), create an intimate, cocoon-like environment, even though the room is open and spacious.

includes the kitchen and living room. A wall of sliding glass doors opens the entire room to the pool and patio. The bedrooms and baths are in the front.

Laura and her husband Vin are excellent examples of community-minded residents who are contributing to the culture and preservation of Key West. As lifelong art collectors, they have currently embraced a new project: the creation of the New Salem Museum and Academy of Fine Art. Located in New Salem, Massachusetts, ninety miles west of Boston, Laura says, "We had been

collecting art for so long that, quite frankly we were running out of room." The museum building, once a boarding school, belonged to Vin's mother and was used infrequently due to its rural location and lack of internet/cable service. Laura says, "She had decided to sell the building, so we purchased it from her and began renovations." She explains, "The collection of art is comprised mostly of work by artists living today and painting in a very technical manner of the old European painters, most falling under the category of 'Contemporary Realism'."

The elegant fabrics create a counterbalance, to the rough coral and gutsy wooden bread bowl holding the still life of marble persimmon.

The couple's mission is to allow the public to access and appreciate the magnificent works being produced today, those typically sold by galleries that go straight to private collections, never to be seen again. The museum will help these living artists by exposing their work to the public, hopefully increasing their marketability, and allowing them to support themselves and their families. Laura and Vin continue to purchase important artwork to include in the museum's permanent collection as well.

A marble bust, found on a trip to Italy, sports a collection of coral necklaces bought from a brocante.

Tall glass doors and outer louvred shutters flank a painting by artist Gregory Mortinson. While on assignment for *National Geographic* in Haiti, he took a photograph and later made the painting of this orphan girl. In her hand is a #2 pencil he had given to her, and because of the painting, she proudly became a celebrity in her little village.

Wrought iron French canopy bed in front bedroom.

A grandfather palm is one of many species of palms surrounding the outdoor area.

A whimsical painting of a French bulldog hangs over the custom-made "toddler's" bathtub in the bathroom. Rooms designed by Laura are never finished without art.

A green "wall" of privacy was created by Craig Reynolds Landscaping, along the pool wall.

AN ENCHANTING HIDEAWAY

Tranquility is the most elusive luxury of all, yet this property was designed to maintain a sense of calm, while surrounded by the energy of Old Town. It celebrates the tropical trees, colors, and textures of Key West, carving out a piece of heaven on a hidden lane just steps from a busy street that leads into town. Before you even see the front of the house, you are engulfed by an overwhelming feeling of being somewhere special. If you speak, it is in a whisper, because you don't want to disturb this all-encompassing environment with its own vibrations. It is a privilege to be here. Being invited into this sanctuary was a confirmation of why I love what I do—finding exceptional places to share with my readers.

When you push open the very heavy, curved-top door, almost like one you'd find at the entrance to a castle, you might just hold your breath while taking in the beauty of the surroundings. It is so secluded and peaceful here that, once you've come through that massive door and find yourself on one of many paths meandering through this magnificent property, you have an inkling of what it might have been like to be Alice in Wonderland. If you were in a hurry to get somewhere, you immediately forget where that somewhere was. This is a place that deserves one's full attention. It was a rare opportunity to be invited in, and an experience to savor.

This enchanted garden was designed and created by Craig Reynolds Landscape Architecture, in tandem with the homeowner, whose good taste and vision for the property is impressive. The property had been neglected for many years by its former owner, but this homeowner must have intuitively known what the property could become with the right landscape designer and creative team for the house. The finished project is remarkably spectacular, not only for its visual impact, but also because of the feelings it invokes. Craig created a seamless connection between the house and the diverse areas of the property.

I decided it would be enlightening to share this talented designer's approach to creating a tropical garden of this magnitude. Toward that end, Craig Reynolds graciously agreed to chat with me in his office overlooking Key West's famed Duval Street.

The homeowner of this property first came to Key West "fourteen years ago, more or less." What attracted him was the acceptance he found in the community. And of course, the sunshine. "Life is lived as a single gift," he said. Before buying the place, this homeowner had rented several houses on the island with his family and, in 2015, bought what he describes as a "very special cottage." I have no doubt that this "house seeker" had an inkling of what this property could become, because when asked what shape it was in, he says, "To describe it as being in rough shape is putting it mildly. The home and property were renovated from the wood frame and dirt up."

The homeowner says, "Latch the gate and the folly of Key West is a thousand miles away. Open the gate and you're a few blocks from art, playhouses, music, dance, dining, and the parade of life."

It took quite a bit of confidence and vision to buy this place, since he admits to not having a clue about what to do with it when he first saw the property. To his credit, he knew to assemble an impressive roster of talented people to create what would become a comfortably low-key, elegant Key West home, seamlessly integrated with a magnificent and extremely special property in the heart of Old Town. It is hard to believe it only took a year and a half to accomplish and the homeowner credits Felicia Campanella Design Architect, Russell Powel Housewright Consultant, Craig Reynolds Landscape Architect, Local Architect, Tom Pope, and Rick Bird Construction with

DESIGNING A TROPICAL GARDEN

Craig Reynolds is a leading landscape architect who has transformed residential properties into exciting and notable environments, creating topographic masterpieces, respectful of their relationship to the locations. For more than eighteen years, Craig has been engaged in all aspects of design and project management for estate gardens throughout South Florida and the Caribbean. He has a clarity of landscape design and creates landscapes that are a unified study in pleasing contrasts. The impact is both disciplined and spontaneous, respectful, and sometimes irreverent. After earning a master's degree in landscape architecture at the University of Florida, Craig worked for seven years in Miami with well-known landscape architect, Raymond Jungles, who was responsible for Craig being in Key West and ultimately opening his own firm here.

When I met with Craig, he was more than generous with his time, and we spoke about gardens in general and specifically about this client's project. He says that in addition to the overall planting design, a garden should seamlessly integrate the hardscape elements (pool, spa, trellis, arbors, patios and decks, fountain, and landscape lighting) with the softscape, making them look is if they have always existed, exactly where you come upon them. To achieve this whole experience, Craig starts by sitting down on the property, walking the property, and listening. He likes to design "from the doors out," within a framework of native plants and indigenous materials. He says, "Each garden is unique and is a collaboration born of the individual site, the architect and the owner's vision or requirements for the property." He feels that the garden is like another room, since it is where Key West residents spend most of their time, and it interacts with the interior of the house.

Examples of different approaches to gardens that Craig has created can be seen throughout this book, notably "An Enchanted Hideaway" and "A Private Oasis." His experience has taught him that the more the homeowners know how they will use the property, the easier it is to design it for their needs. He also says that gardens change, with seasons and growth, which can be exciting as well as requiring constant maintenance, especially in the tropics. This is something to take into consideration when planning your garden.

A winding stone pathway meanders to the front door of the cottage—if you don't get lost in the interconnecting spaces along the way. Sunlight seeps through the palm trees, magnifying their grandeur.

Large pavers let you stroll to the back pool with all sorts of beckoning detours. Everything here is designed for visual and sensual experiences. It is a reminder to slow down and enjoy being here.

its success. As I learned more about the property, it was clear that this homeowner was incredibly modest about the influence he brought to the project, giving his full attention and creative input to every detail with impeccable sensitivity. The confluence of talents is personified in the finished project. It is very exciting to see what is possible.

When asked what he likes most about living here, he said, "This house provides a feeling of warmth and safety," But like most residents, he has one pet peeve—the iguanas. "It's the biggest challenge," he admits. It's the garden that gives him the most pleasure. "Craig Reynolds created a secret garden, a daydream. The gate is the morning blanket you pull over your eyes to delay reality."

The house is just a few feet away, but completely hidden from view until it's right in front of you. It has a clear and strong relationship to nature and is interconnected to the site.

The front door opens directly into the living room from which all other rooms are accessed. All the rooms are nicely proportioned, creating the comfortable feeling of a warm, traditional family home.

The side door leads into the homeowner's office, directly facing the pool.

The pool was designed to fit neatly into the landscaping as if it's always been there. The outdoor shower is in a grotto-like quarry, as luxurious as it gets. Objects of art come into view, tucked here and there into the landscape, never obvious.

The hammock provides the perfect spot for an afternoon snooze.

Shiplap covers walls in the small, perfectly designed kitchen, surrounded by a wall of greenery.

The homeowner's office looks out onto the lush greenery surrounding the pool and patio.

The primary bedroom is on the second floor where the curves of the ceiling, the antique furniture, the soft blue colors of the walls and textures create the feeling of being on a luxury cruise ship. The chandelier is a Key West touch.

Opposite wall of the kitchen with built-in cupboards, a farmhouse sink, and retro fittings. The walls are painted with just the right hint of ice blue. The "barely there" paint colors used throughout the house, are subdued, rich, low-key and absolutely right for where they are used.

The bathroom is the personification of pure luxury; a soaking tub has its own alcove with treetop views.

"TRIP TO HEAVEN"

Kate Hoffman-Brown and her extended family have been coming to Key West for years. There are Kate's four kids, lots of siblings, nieces, and nephews, and everyone is always welcome. Kate has created a relaxed home where family and friends casually drop by. There's nothing precious here. It's a "kick off your shoes and hang out for a while" kind of home. Kate was just coming back from a walk with a friend when we arrived. She said, "The only reason any of us came here, was because of my brother Trip. He was responsible for getting the family to Key West and the house is named in his honor. Trip was a charismatic Key West icon."

"The best streets in Old Town are Margaret, William, and Elizabeth. There are no other comparable streets." Trip used to say. And he knew what he was talking about.

I met Trip Hoffman in 1990. He was "the go-to guy" for real estate. He knew just how to match people with homes. He had good taste and style and knew everyone else who shared his aesthetics. Trip Hoffman decorated all the good houses in Key West and his interior design style was personal, inventive, and sophisticated, yet at the same time homey. Trip loved a good yard sale. Perhaps Kate has picked up on this inviting home style. Over the years, no matter when we'd cross paths, Trip Hoffman remained enthusiastic about the community of Key West and its houses.

Kate's house was originally built in 1890 and renovated ten years ago. It sits high above the street level, affording that rare sense of privacy

Kate's pup "Trout" has a front row seat from her bicycle basket.

in Old Town. What Kate has managed to do in a very small footprint is to fit a decent-size bedroom and bath upstairs that opens onto a balcony overlooking the deck and pool, a luxurious guest bedroom at the back of the first floor, that opens onto the deck and pool areas, and a small sitting room in the front to the left of the entryway.

The second-floor balcony and downstairs bedroom look out over the private back deck and pool.

There's also a guest cottage at the other end of the pool. Kate has gotten the most out of a small lot and has managed to make room for everyone. And by the way, the house is on one of the three streets that were Trip's favorites. "When it came up for sale," Kate said, "I knew I had to buy it."

A lovely blue and white art glass vase is filled with pink roses to spice up the color scheme.

Even though the houses are quite close, there's a sense of privacy. The pool/guest house is to the left.

The front door opens into the living room where you're met by a riot of yellow and blue, and all sorts of interesting objects and furniture. Michael helped Kate pick out the furnishings and make the place homey. The painting is by Lance Berry.

Looking down from the upstairs balcony.

One expects to find orchids clinging to trees in a Key West yard, whether humble or grand.

The kitchen is almost a passageway to the back deck and cocktail pool. Restored Dade County pine gives this room character. Fresh fruit and nuts are an easy grab on the way in or out. In Key West no pool is too tiny.

COMFORTABLE ON ASHE STREET

Like many of the streets in town, Ashe Street was named after one of its early settlers, Thomas J. Ashe, one of the city's first engineers. This street borders Old Town where the houses are typically wood-framed Conch cottages.

Don Desrosiers and Will Dewey first came to Key West in the late 1980s and are not novices to house renovations, having owned and restored three houses, all in Old Town, before buying this one seven years ago. The location and one-floor living are what attracted the couple to buy this house. Over the years they and their now-grown daughters, Katie and Libbie, have made Key West their second home. Don says, "The girls have been coming here since they were infants."

Don and Will divide their time between Key West and Newport, Rhode Island, where they have been in the hospitality business their entire careers. Their inn, the Francis Malbone House, is an imposing eighteenth-century, meticulously restored retreat in the heart of Newport's harbor front district.

"We love the diversity, charm, and walkability of Key West, and Old Town in particular," Don says. "When we bought this house the systems and the house itself had been well-maintained, but very dated." They put in a new kitchen, and bathrooms as well as a new pool, new flooring on the porch, and exposed the Dade County pine interior walls. "What attracted us most to this house were the wraparound porches and the great light that came in everywhere."

With the help of their longtime friend, decorator Michael Pelkey, they have created a home that is timeless and elegant, with color and textiles that bring the house to life. It is equally inviting for casual lounging or large-scale entertaining and exudes a quiet sophistication and warmth that responds perfectly to this family's refined and easy lifestyle.

It was built in 1928, but there were no old photographs to reference, no history to refer to. With the goal of wanting the house to evolve organically, they decided to live in it for a season in order to determine what they wanted to accomplish before taking on a major remodeling. The project took three years to complete. The biggest challenge they had was to maintain an authentic Key West cottage and not destroy the historic importance of the house. Toward that end they kept the Cuban tile floors wherever possible and exposed several Dade County pine interior walls. Don says, "We love the flow of the house from the porches through to the pool and garden, all on the same plane."

This family especially appreciates the location of the house because it affords walkability to most places and is bikeable to everything. "Our first house was on Francis Street across from the cemetery where we taught the girls how to ride a bike."

The pink Conch cottage is separated from the street by a wide porch, lush gardens, and a neatly painted picket fence. The gingerbread trim is typical on rooflines of these little cottages seen throughout Old Town.

Don and Will have seamlessly become part of the community and support the arts and theater. "There is a great food scene here," they say, "from basic to high end." However, when asked, they couldn't name a favorite restaurant because, they said, "We love so many of them."

The front porch is a favorite morning hangout surrounded by tropical gardens created by local landscape architect, Carl Gilley. The painted ceiling color is called "haint blue" and dates back to the descendants of the Gullah Geechee of Central and West African slaves. They painted the porch ceilings to keep away "haints" or spirits. The color is also rumored to trick wasps and insects into thinking the ceiling is the sky, driving them away from porch sitters.

The flow from the front door through to the back deck is quite dramatic. The renovation involved preserving original Dade County pine that casts a warm glow over the rooms.

When it came to furnishing the house they said, "Michael understands the vibe we wanted to maintain. He's worked with us on all four houses we renovated here, and on several projects in Newport." They were definite about not wanting their Key West home to have a "Northern" feel.

While the house is tastefully decorated, it is not precious. It has that relaxed feeling that family homes usually take years to acquire. It is layered with subtle, but carefully curated textures, art, and collectibles with a back story. Artists represented throughout the house are:

A wall of Haitian art adds lively color on a narrow living room wall. A shell-encrusted box and orchid sit on a table under the front windows.

The main bedroom is fired up with just the right splashes of orange and the perfect counterbalance of early black and white framed photos filling the wall above the bed.

Michael Palmer, Christos Colivas, Tom Dickson, and Evelyn Boren.

This house says, "Sit down, make yourself comfortable, and don't be in a hurry to leave." Toward that end, this couple enjoys the porch in the early morning, cocktail hour by the pool, and they love making dinner for friends. The flow of the house is perfect for social gatherings inside or out, depending on the weather. Will, who went to cooking school, is a marvelous chef, and whips up a meal for friends that is always highly anticipated. This property personifies "of the moment," upscale Key West casual.

Rattan chairs encircle the round dining room table for intimate dinners on chilly evenings. Pieces of coral are displayed on the wall shelves.

All rooms open to this inviting pool where friends are always welcome. Carl Gilley planted tropical palms with a nod toward a Key West "well-groomed" landscape that isn't overly manicured.

The table is set for a poolside brunch with guests. Outdoor living and entertaining is casual, but always celebratory. It's a Key West thing to make every gathering fun.

A one-room guest cottage sits at the edge of the deck surrounding the pool. Carl Gilley planted a natural wall of tropical plants and trees to create a private oasis in the heart of town. Outdoor fabric allows for luxury without worry. Pillows and cushions are impervious to the occasional and sudden tropical downpour, intense but brief.

The front doors of the sunny yellow facade open into the large (by Key West standards) kitchen of Casa Sapodilla, named for the exotic tropical trees on the property. The Sapodilla is a long-lived evergreen tree native to southern Mexico, Central America, and the Caribbean.

CASA SAPODILLA

Fran Decker and her husband came to Key West on a vacation in 1975, but it wasn't until 1988 that they decided to make Key West their home. They could have lived anywhere in the world, having traveled to many romantic, interesting, and exotic places. As it happened, they were completing a three-year sail around the Caribbean and Central America and thinking about where to settle. Key West had the warm weather year-round, as well as that laid-back Caribbean lifestyle, and it was located in the United States. "We bought our house in 2005 after living in Marathon Key, on Flamingo Island for seventeen years," Fran said. The sprawling Sapodilla trees that sit rather majestically on the property may have had some influence on that decision. Fran says the big porches were another attraction.

Fran is an artist, former gallery owner, and newly appointed Queen of Fantasy Fest. She joined the island Arts Co-op in 2001, then along with five partners, opened SoDu Gallery in 2006. Four years later she opened the Frangipani Gallery on Duval Street, and later merged the two. The galleries were so successful she was spending all her time on bookkeeping and less on making art. Ultimately, she gave up the gallery so she could spend all her time painting. She is very much involved with the art community in Key West and her work can be found at many galleries around the island.

Fran says, "The original building dates back to 1870 and was once an apartment and office complex owned by Dr. Herman Moore." She adds, "Although this house looks old, it was rebuilt in

1996 and was in move-in condition." As an artist, Fran particularly liked the spice color scheme of the paint in all the rooms, so she kept it. It went with her Caribbean Island sensibility.

The house is informed by the couple's many trips to exotic places. It is filled with layers of memories. "We went to Bali to purchase furniture for the house," she says. "When we returned, we knew we wanted to create a pool like those we saw there, tucked naturally into rock formations." Toward that end, the first thing the couple did

Purple shutters, the cutout of the Sapodilla leaves, a funky rooster, lounging mermaid, and imposing Buddha announce the playful and artistic nature of this homeowner.

Fran's cats sit in the dining alcove.

The living room is a riot of color and African masks, layers of textures, and a giant carved crocodile is used as a wooden coffee table.

was to remove one of the two driveways in order to renovate and enlarge a very plain lap pool, turning it into a tropical oasis with three rock waterfalls. They also added a large hot tub in a rock formation.

Now the side of the house, accessed from the living room, provides an outdoor room that is visually pleasing, with the addition of soft sounds from the trickling water, and sun seeping through the wall of palm trees. This natural "fence"

provides privacy from neighboring houses and the surrounding comings and goings on this lovely Old Town street. The most recent garden renovation was done right after Hurricane Irma in 2018 by one of Key West's premier landscape designers, Patrick Tierney (now deceased).

Especially interesting is the unusual floor plan with two separate unconnected upstairs areas. "It gives everyone their privacy," she explained. Fran

The back porch is a peaceful spot to relax on the rattan chaise lounges with the sound of the water fountain and the pool just steps away. The metal drum table is from India and the lamp is made from Cypress root from the Everglades, topped with a handwoven shade.

The pool and hot tub were created to look like they are in a lagoon and have always been there. The couple designed this oasis based on those they saw in Bali. The wall of palm trees separates this property from the tightly knit neighboring houses, so common in Old Town. (*See sidebar with tips for maintaining a tropical garden*)

is thinking of creating an orchid oasis but says, "I have to get rid of the resident iguanas first." Iguanas are relatively harmless, but they do feed on vegetation and can be quite messy.

Every room is filled with an impressive collection of art and artifacts from around the world as

well as from local Keys artists whose work Fran has admired over the years: Jim Salem, John Martini, William Welch, Andy Thurber, David Scott Meier, Rick Worth, Susann D'Antonio, Deborah Moore, Gail Upmal, Martha DePoo, Neva Townsend,

Abigail White, Pam Eden, Barb Grob, Judy Bradford, Sonia Robinson, Karen Beauprie, and many others. Her eclectic collections prove that sophistication and fun aren't mutually exclusive.

Fran has favorite places in the house at different times. "I love the porches, both upstairs and down, and I spend a lot of time in the comfortable living room." But then she considers the bedroom with its four-poster bed and sunny nook and, for a moment, that's her favorite place.

Fran says, "Key West is my heart home. Despite the dangers of hurricanes and global warming, I plan to be in Key West forever, because I have yet to find a place I'd rather be." And this is saying a lot, coming from someone who has traveled the world.

One of many whimsical figures hidden in plain sight throughout the property.

The plaque says it all.

TRIED AND TRUE TIPS FOR MAINTAINING A TROPICAL GARDEN

Kenny Weschler came to Key West from New York City where he had been maintaining gardens, if not tropical ones, for many years. He has spent nearly three decades maintaining tropical gardens throughout Key West and says, "The foliage may differ, but the rules of the road apply everywhere." I have lived in over twenty-five houses in Key West and Kenny seemed to be the gardener who maintained most of the gardens. We have been friends for many years, and several years ago I included his house in one of my books. So, it was his expertise that I sought out for some simple, direct advice that might be applied to gardens wherever you live.

Size Doesn't Matter

Visualize your new plant or shrub in a year or even three. It's always sad to have to remove a relatively new specimen because it has outgrown and crowded out your overall garden.

No Last-Minute Pruning

Keep your plants and shrubs in check. Prune a little at a time. Don't be a last-minute hacker. Nothing is more noticeable than the overzealous hack because you are expecting guests.

Sun and Shade

Know which of your plants prefer or require full to moderate sunlight. On the other hand, many plants thrive only in shaded areas. Read the label or ask your nursery maven.

Irrigation

In subtropical climates such as ours, an irrigation system is a must. It doesn't need to be elaborate, but it must provide complete coverage and have a day-of-week and timing mechanism. This is true with every garden, especially if it will be left to fend for itself for months at a time. And remember, even if you live in the tropics full-time, you will not be able to keep up the watering with a garden hose!

The Big View

Whatever size your garden is, view it as a tapestry. Think about scale, placement, and texture of each entry. And, most importantly, leave some "negative" or vacant space. When gardens start growing, the clarity will get lost unless space is provided for from the beginning.

Last Reminder

You don't get a second chance to make a first impression! Your garden is what people see first. Make it the very best you can!

COZY AND COMPACT

Tucked away in a little enclave of tiny cottages, this neat three-room home is perfect for Terje Stenstad, who spends the winter months in Key West, the other months in his hometown of Oslo, Norway. "Summer lasts about three weeks there," he says, explaining why he chose to buy a home in Key West.

"I like to say that Donna Summer, my all-time favorite artist, brought me to Key West," he answered when asked how he came to buy a house here. "I went to see her in concert in Orlando in March of 2004. It was my first visit back to Florida in 26 years. I traveled from there to Miami and had a couple of extra days to spend. I had heard of this place called Key West and wanted to explore it." Terje (pronounced "Tahd-ja") rented a convertible and fell deeply in love as each mile brought him closer to this tropical city at the tip of Florida.

"When I arrived, the love affair had officially started," he adds. He only spent one night here but was determined to return the following year. Terje rented a house for six months and spent most of his time writing what became a best-selling children's book in Norway. Many more successful books followed.

Key West homeowners are interesting people. They come here from all over the world, creating a fascinating mix of cultures. Like many before him, what attracted Terje most about Key West was the weather. "I was born and raised above the Arctic Circle, in the northern part of Norway,"

A birthday celebration under the avocado tree.

he says. Being cold all the time was an assumed fact of life. "In Key West I can walk to town in flip flops, see the sun all year long and not be cold."

This little cottage, built in the late 1800s, had just been rebuilt when he purchased it in 2009. He had previously rented three different houses. "I absolutely love this little cottage, perched on Solares Hill, the highest point on the island." The

A colorful, bungalow-style, three-room cottage on Solares Hill, the highest point in Key West.

house was move-in ready, but this new home-owner added custom shelving, one of which is built into the living room wall. He installed a wall of sliding glass doors leading from the living room to the deck that spans the back of this barely 500 square foot cottage. "It has made my living space three times as big," he says.

Over the years, Terje has put what he calls "the necessary love" into it. He points out the avocado tree is his treasure. He planted it from a seed, and the landscaping he's lovingly perfected over the years has grown into mature plantings very quickly. "Last year this tree yielded 75 large avocados," he proudly boasts.

The back of the house contains a compact but adequate pocket of a kitchen, and living room that's as wide as the house and opens to the deck.

Terje likes small spaces and the compact living that became popular in Scandinavia in the nineties. "I come from a place where I'm used to thinking smart about small spaces," he explains. He knew immediately how he could make the most of this cottage. "Where I come from, interior décor, for the most part, is white, light wood colors, and no fun!" he says. "Bright colors make me happy." Living here only part-time, he appreciates the ease with which he can turn the key and leave.

The house was originally owned by John Burbine and Stephanie Bartley. "The day I moved in, they came over with a bottle of champagne and it ignited a great friendship," Another reminder of the prevailing community spirit of Key West.

Old Town appealed to this single homeowner because of its charm and its proximity to all fun

The front door opens into a narrow hallway that leads to the back of the house, much the way the original shotgun houses were built.

This Norwegian soup tureen and salt and pepper shakers are from the seventies. Terje remembers them from his childhood cabin. The saying, "If you want to taste it all you have to taste the sour and the salt." And another Norwegian homily, often inscribed on pepper shakers, is "Pepper in food puts pep into the soul."

things to do. He says, "I never get tired of going for walks or bike rides around the island." He loves the island vibe and says he tends to spend as much time outdoors as possible. "In Norway, we live most of the time indoors. In the last year my career and life have shifted, and I find this is a great place to write, both indoors and out."

Key West has provided him with the dream life he didn't know he craved and he's very grateful to be able to live two parallel lives. "I don't need a lot to be happy. This house is compact, easy and convenient. It has a definite calming effect." And being the gregarious sort that he is, Terje knows everyone in the neighborhood.

For many years this was the place he'd go to get away from a busy career in Norway, where he was a show producer with a production company starring many of Norway's biggest names in music and comedy.

When Covid hit, it gave him time to reflect on what he had achieved, which led to his selling the company. With the freedom to create his own path, Terje has turned to writing full-time. "It's the most difficult thing I've ever done, " he says, "but also the most rewarding." Creative challenges don't seem to faze this entrepreneur. Could it be a Norwegian thing?

The deck doubles the indoor space and is surrounded by a fence and a lush, manageable garden. The tropical outdoor pillows are by artist Dawn Wilkins, whose paintings are represented at Art@830 on Caroline Street.

THE ORCHID HOUSE

Due to the overwhelming profusion of orchids in the front of this house, it is perhaps one of the most photographed properties in Old Town. To the current owners' credit, they have kept up the stewardship and love sitting on the front porch watching people stop to photograph the orchids. "Our two golden retrievers love the house as much as we do," they say. "The younger one, Zoey, loves to greet all the passersby. She has more friends than we do," they admit.

The owners of this house had previously owned another house on the same street, and they say, "It was a total re-do and we sold it the day we put it on the market." Ralph Firestone and Gary Merriman retired very early from careers in the medical profession to enjoy doing the things they love, dividing their time between Key West and their "access-only-by-boat" home in one of the Thousand Island's area of Ontario, Canada. They say, "We lived in Central New York for our entire careers and raised our three children there."

These homeowners are not new to Key West and, like so many, bought a house here after spending two to three weeks vacationing on the island. They were immediately attracted to the laid-back lifestyle. They bought this house in 2014 and say it was in very good condition. "We only had to do a few things to make it our own." This "only a few things" involved painting inside and out, redoing the pool, and adding an awning over the back decks, lighting, landscape changes, and

THERE'S SOMETHING ABOUT ORCHIDS!

What is it about orchids that make us smile? In Victorian-era society, few possessions surpassed orchids as status symbols. Collectors prized their rarity as much as their exotic charm. In Key West, most certainly due to the consistently perfect weather conducive to their growing and thriving, orchids are ubiquitous all over the island. They cling to trees; they are found in pots on porches and they always add life and beauty to interior rooms.

Exotic plants fill the yard.

The owners' two golden retrievers love to watch people admiring the profusion of orchids that define the landscaping in front of this house.

The front porch is all about the profusion of fuchsia pink. The porch provides a front row seat to the world beyond the front yard and embodies the luxury of time.

houses on the street, that it was built in the mid 1890s. It was their intent to bring in their own style, without destroying the charm of the house. "We spend six or more months in this house and love the lifestyle we experience here," they say. Favorite pastimes are walking through Old Town in the morning, working on the house and garden, relaxing poolside, and visiting favorite restaurants and wine bars. They love sharing the house with out-of-town guests, as they were doing on the day we arrived. They were also in the throes of planning a Key West wedding for one of their offspring that would take place in the spring.

Growing orchids in the tropics is irresistible.

remodeling a bathroom. The project was complete within a year. Having lived down the street, they always admired this house and knew exactly what they would do when they finally bought it. "We were always attracted to its charm, and we loved the front porch." Set back from the street and enclosed by a white picket fence and, of course, all those arresting orchids, provide a buffer from the inevitable photo seekers on this busy street.

While the homeowners don't know the exact age of the house, they believe, based on other

The dining area table is adorned with a "still-life creation" from coral, shells, and tropical fruits. To the left is a sitting alcove for morning coffee when it's too cold to sit outside.

The biggest challenge they faced when remodeling the house was the bathroom. "It was a total gut job," they say. "We had to move the location of the fixtures and redo the plumbing. We also had to replace the entrance door to the bedroom with French doors that now lead out to the front porch."

When asked what overall feeling they've created in the house they say, "Warmth." These homeowners support the arts and have paintings

by many local artists including Alan Maltz, Charles Lee, a contemporary Korean artist, and Amanda Johnson. Aside from the front porch, these homeowners love the little alcove in the living room. "It's tucked in with a couple of chairs and an ottoman and it's the perfect spot to enjoy our morning coffee while reading the newspaper." But then they quickly add, "Mostly we are outside on the front porch or in the backyard poolside—in the dead of winter!" That's the ultimate draw to Key West, especially when your other home is in the northern part of the country.

The bathroom was completely remodeled and is sleek, modern, and functional.

One of two imposing front bedrooms is filled with optimistic colors, patterns, and textures, as well as local art and a model shrimp boat.

Left: The owners love their matching Vespas for scooting around town.

This is where the couple and their guests spend most of their time. It's completely private with a fence and plantings on all sides. A wall of mirrors on the fence enlarges the feel of the space.

CHOOSING THE "RIGHT" COLOR PALETTE

Lately one finds fewer colorfully painted rooms and shades of white or gray are still trending and probably will be around for some time, because it's easy to live with and is a good background for colorful furnishings and art. The "haint" blue used for porch ceilings can be achieved with Sherwin Williams "Waterscape," a soft blue infused with hints of green. The color depends on the natural light on your porch and the greenery surrounding your house. But this color blends beautifully. Another is Palladian Blue from Benjamin Moore or Borrowed Light from Farrow and Ball. Consider Benjamin Moore's Paper White, that has a crisp, clean, perfect "barely there" hint of gray. The walls of the Orchid House are painted with Benjamin Moore's White Dove and Chantilly Lace trim. This is a good background for art, not too cool or gray. Designers call it the most "barely there" color. Athena is a softer white, the perfect light griege.

The Conch cottage sits right up to the sidewalk, separated only by a narrow yard and picket fence. The front of this house retains the original exterior siding, vintage hurricane shutters, and a tin roof. A bougainvillea afire in shocking pink provides a dramatic welcome.

HIGH ON THE HILL

This is a town of six degrees of separation. There is a very efficient telegraph system, the Coconut Telegraph, that sends messages to the community, much like a town crier of yore. If something is worth repeating, and often when it is not, everyone at the Old Town Bakery or the Cuban Coffee Queen or someone in the post office knows about it. Nothing is a secret. So it was probably inevitable that Jill Gudoian would buy a house in Key West.

Jill came to Key West on a family visit in 2002 and fell in love with those tangible and elusive qualities that never fail to work their magic. Over the years she rented different vacation homes throughout Old Town. Her longtime friends from Newport, Rhode Island, Will and Don (see page 37), started on a campaign to convince her to buy a home here. "They thought it was more practical for me to buy," she says. She would choose a house in a neighborhood that, when you sneeze, the telegraph system jumps to attention.

So, in March of 2013 she purchased a little Conch cottage, originally built in 1924.

The house sits close to the front sidewalk in this tightly woven area known as Solares Hill. It is the highest point on the island and the houses are a conglomeration of simply built, unpretentious, for the most part small wooden homes, lining each side of Elizabeth Street. You can't miss anything going on in front of your house.

When Jill first saw the house, it screamed "total renovation," or maybe "gut job." It needed a reconfiguration of the layout. The kitchen, bathroom, bedrooms, and living room all needed to

The upstairs guest bedroom.

The side door leads right into the living room. In the front of the house are two bedrooms and a bathroom. Everything is shipshape. Carefully planned built-in shelving holds a display of early pudding molds, shell boxes, and other objects of interest, sourced for Jill by Michael Pelkey.

be renovated, updated, and reconfigured to make it livable. "The biggest challenge," she says, "was configuring the second-floor bathroom within the limited space up there." Today the bedroom and compact bathroom create a bright, private aerie. Jill hired Ben Teague Designs to do the interior design. The gardens in the back around the pool were designed by Rob Creider, Just Keys Trees.

Looking from the living room into the dining room. The painting, "Summer Sun" is by Rhode Island artist Chris Wyllie.

Jill found this fanciful sign for the kitchen at a long gone shop on Southard Street.

Jill likes to entertain her friends and sets a lively table in the open living/dining room with easy access to the well-designed kitchen. Occasionally, she joins Will and Don around their pool with their good friend Michael Pelkey. This town is interconnected and the very thing that makes it so much fun to be here. There's always something going on and friends to share it with.

Tropical trees create a dense wall of privacy around the small pool and in-town property. We call these cocktail pools for dipping your toes while holding a drink.

The interior is layered with a healthy dose of playfulness: bright colors and some touches of tongue-in-cheek. Clever ideas abound. A serious approach to decorating this house would be incongruous with the overall vibe of the island, this house, and this homeowner. Jill loves the neighborhood, finds the house the perfect fit for herself and her two kids and it feels instantly liveable and inviting. She says she has wonderful neighbors, the area is quiet, and, when she's not on her bike (like most of us, she doesn't use a car in Key West), she can walk anywhere in five minutes.

DANISH TWIST

Geography plays a big part in community. The houses in Old Town have their individual stories, but collectively they tell a bigger tale. You can almost imagine neighbors sharing gossip over fences barely separating properties. You know they knew everything about each other's lives. That is community, and it continues. The people who lived in Old Town long ago walked through these same streets and lanes that border the cemetery, where many generations of a family might be buried. Old Town is steeped in the history of Key West and is the backbone of the community.

Bordering on a lane and the Key West cemetery, this shaded lot has the distinction of a rare and ancient ficus tree in the front yard. Another distinguishing factor is that the house is composed of two side-by-side cottages that became one home. The front porch spans the width of the house and sitting here is like having a front row seat to the best show in town. There's a leisurely pace in this most coveted section of Old Town. The mature plantings and bordering cemetery create a hush and a feeling of space where properties are close together.

"What made you buy a house in another country and particularly Key West?" I asked the owners.

"We wanted to find a place where you could wear shorts in the winter," these industrial designers from Denmark said, as one of the homeowners raced out in shorts, t-shirt, and flip-flops to go teach a Zumba dance class.

When you enter the house, the drama of the space, and the relationship to the surrounding property, is breathtaking. This home is a celebration of craftsmanship and a stage for edgy contemporary design. It simultaneously alludes to the past while celebrating what is possible now. The garden surrounding the house plays its part in this integrated design—at once inside and out at the same time. This property is an experience that offers a rare glimpse into a Key West you might not have known existed.

The treated wood walls and ceiling, made from California pine oak, create a feeling of shelter—an exquisite contrast to the surrounding landscape seen from wherever you are. This is a home that exudes a sense of imagination. The renovation balances the best of modern technology and building techniques with the finest craftsmanship, and attention to detail that comes about when architecture and landscape design are perfectly aligned. It is almost impossible to imagine this much property in back of what you see facing the street, and how perfectly married it is to the interior.

These homeowners came from Denmark to Key West in February 2009. They explained, "Our initial search for a winter home started in Cape Town, South Africa where we already had friends.

The ficus tree is the main attraction in the front yard of this double-wide house.

The living room is a tightly edited selection of furnishings with white trim and furniture balanced against a background of the warm wood of the walls and floor.

The porch spans the entire house and provides a front row seat to the best ongoing show in town. The black and white cushions are as neat and crisp as the interior furnishings.

This wonderful beehive-shaped fireplace is original to the house. As you can imagine, there aren't many fireplaces in Key West.

In the end we decided against it and looked again at the globe for a place with the same language and modern infrastructure. South Florida, and Key West in particular, stood out. It immediately felt like home."

The house was built around 1935 and was in terrible condition. "The construction was just the termites holding hands," they joked. The couple lived in the house for almost four years before feeling confident to spend money on the make-over. The new construction was planned with the local architectural firm of Bender and Associates Architects who, because of the homeowners' backgrounds, were able to work together. Due to the city's preservation rules, they had to keep a central part of the old house footprint. Wood that could be salvaged was combined with new material. That added up to a few pieces of construction wood, some outside cladding, three windows, and something rare for Key West, a brick fireplace, "the rarity making up for its lack of prettiness," they said. Once they got started, the renovation took about a year. The finished home reflects the homeowner's informed imagination, balanced with the best of modern technology, the finest craftsmanship and attention to detail that comes when the right talents work together on a challenging project.

A compact bathroom makes good use of small space, designed with the efficiency of the inside of a ship.

A wall of glass reveals those spectacular views, ever-changing with the light and the time of day.

The spacious design incorporates an office, living room, kitchen, small bedroom, and compact bathroom. "We don't spend much time in the bedroom so we thought making that a large room wouldn't be prudent." But everyone knows that when you have a house in Key West, and your friends and family live in cold weather, you will always have guests—especially when they live in another country, and one that is quite cold in the winter. The guest house across the pool at the far side of the property solved the problem, enabling everyone to have privacy and to experience this fabulous property.

The homeowners said, "There is a very distinct style in these old American houses. In Denmark, brick houses tend to be more the norm. We wanted to create a home that felt like it has been there for a long time. You'll notice about old houses, they evolve over time, get reshuffled and added onto. That's what gives them oddity and charm. So we created a 'story' about three separate buildings that have been joined. The buildings have an outside cladding of white painted board and batten

Everything functional in the kitchen is hidden across one end of the room. The table and chairs were custom made.

and an inside of rich, dark wood. As you walk from room to room, you sense the mix of white and dark walls and everything makes sense, design-wise because of the story."

"Like the house," they continued, "we wanted the property at the back of the house to look like it has always been there. We felt the pool should look like a building feature that could have been here for a long time. It might have been repurposed from an earlier use. Maybe it was an abandoned industrial basin, filled with rainwater and overgrown with plants." It leaves room for imagination. The one thing they wanted was an "honest" pool.

A leopard-pattern carpeted hallway leads to the homeowners' office. The portrait was made from cut papers and applied with découpage.

The pool sits in the middle of the property between the house and guest cottage, affording visiting guests a different perspective of the landscape design.

A brick path leads around the pool where the guest cottage is nestled into the landscape. It has been designed as a miniature of the main house.

By now we had photographed enough properties to recognize the work of Craig Reynolds. When Craig talks about his work you pick up on his reverence for the natural beauty of the tropics. He feels it's important to plan a garden with indigenous plants appropriate for the site. (See more about tropical gardens on p. 26.)

The room that gives these designers the most pleasure is the kitchen. It has space enough to walk around, have conversations, cook, do creative work, and hang out with friends. "Honestly," they say, "we have been so lucky to be adopted into an existing group of friends." They admit it was not planned, but is unimaginable not to have them in their lives. "Finding your kind of people, especially in a foreign country, is rare. This is now our Key West family," they say. And when I asked, "What one word defines the feel of your home?" they said, "Harmonious." Many different elements work together here to form a pleasingly consistent whole. This is the new Key West panache.

The house sits at the back of the property. The "courtyard" and the shallow pond with a fountain, surrounded by a tropical garden, create a serene and supremely private environment in this close neighborhood in Old Town.

A PRIVATE OASIS

I first saw this house several years ago, when it was on the Key West House and Garden tour. I thought it was the perfect house for Key West. It reminded me of a Parisian apartment because of the tall glass doors and exquisite hardware. I loved the big open room from which everything emanated. I loved the deep cushioned window seat that ran the width of the room under a bank of windows filled with palm trees that changed their colors with the light. This was a home I could live in. And I have been in hundreds of great homes. For several years I have kept a snapshot of the living room on my desktop. It is labeled, "my fave house." So I was incredibly excited when Tamara said she was photographing the garden for Craig Reynolds and insisted that we put it in the book. It was the last house we shot, after we thought the book was finished. But how could I miss this opportunity? (As it turned out, we could have gone on and on with many more wonderful houses.) This is a gem. It is unusual in Old Town for the property to be in the front of the house.

When we arrived, we opened the gate that led into a little brick area surrounded by tropical plantings. It had been designed for parking bikes. Living in Old Town is conducive to biking everywhere and these lifelong New Yorkers are no exception. Everyone arrives by bicycle. Once our bikes were secure, we followed the winding brick path to what the homeowners call the courtyard. This large piece of property presents a dramatic approach to the house that sits at the back of the property, proudly overseeing the gardens, the

Looking out the front doors. Living is easy here.

The living room, with its simple, well-designed furniture is an all-purpose room where work, working out, relaxing, reading, and casually seeing friends are all easily accommodated.

Double wood-framed glass doors span the width of the house and offer the opportunity for adjusting the exposure to the outdoors.

The tiny but efficient kitchen is tucked into the back corner of the house. Kitchens do not tend to be large in Key West. They sometimes seem like an afterthought.

trickling fountain and reflecting pond, and the entire area between the house and the street. The wide, covered porch across the front of the house is perfect for enjoying any meal alfresco. It was one of the main attributes the homeowners saw in the house, and where they spend most of their time when they are here. But it was the outdoor courtyard that had them hooked.

The house is quite different from others on the street. It was built circa 1991 and feels urban modern by Key West standards. It would be at home in a European city. The homeowners came to Key West fifteen years ago just for the week-end. In 2016 they bought this house. It was in good condition, only needing a paint job and a new garden, which in all took just three months to complete. These homeowners knew what they wanted: one is an architect, the other a museum director, and they worked with Craig Reynolds to create the gardens. The result feels at once disci-plined and spontaneous. "A garden should look and feel like it's always been there," Craig says.

"It reminded us of Caribbean 'island hous-es'," the homeowners said. "We were especially

attracted to the high ceilings, the great light and the wide front porch overlooking the entire property."

There are three tall, double doors that open to the porch. The overall feeling of the interior design is relaxed and speaks to the couple's life-style. The furnishings are simple, purposeful, and well-designed. The light wood furniture contrasts beautifully with the white painted wood floors and the soft hues. There is a small, almost unno-ticeable kitchen tucked into the back of the house, and to each side of the front doors that span the central living room are two separate bedroom and bathroom suites. Craig created a garden wall and a trickling fountain outside the couple's bedroom windows to soothe the senses. When they are in Key West, they say they work and work out and the house is a good place for both.

I spoke with landscape architect Craig Rey-nolds about the garden design. He said, "when they bought this property, the garden had been destroyed by Hurricane Irma, leaving no priva-cy. You could see the house fully exposed from the street. The most important thing for this couple was to create privacy. They wanted a garden entrance that played off the symmetry of the property. Toward that end we relocated two lignum vitae trees to create an archway and there are two paths that converge and guide you to the front of what is now the courtyard, like a little plaza with a shallow reflecting pond and a fountain. The pleasing sound of trickling water is always present. The mahogany tree was already there; all the hardscape is new." The garden, surrounding the courtyard includes seven vari-eties of palm trees, as well as native crab woods

Craig designed a garden pathway on the side of the house and created a fountain in front of a garden wall.

A potted air plant sits on the front porch.

and bay rum trees that are kept trim. The smell is intoxicating. But that "aha" moment comes when you wind your way down the garden path. The vista opens up, and there you are, transport-ed to a secluded landscape, completely buffered from the comings and goings of everyday life in Old Town. The variety of mature plantings makes it impossible to believe that the property hasn't always looked this way. The house is centered at the back of the property, surrounded by plantings of different shades of green. This was designed to draw the eye to the house. Asked for one word to describe their home and the homeowners say, "Serene." And for just a little while, we were privi-leged to share the experience.

ELEGANT RETREAT FOR ONE

"I live, eat, and breathe real estate," Brenda Donnelly states emphatically. As a busy real estate agent, she specializes in Old Town and Casa Marina. Brenda came to Key West from Pennsylvania in 1981. Of course, she was attracted by the weather, but also the art community. She admits to being a "very" amateur painter and says she paints for herself and for relaxation. Aside from a busy career she loves living in this little compound. "This unit was designed for the owner of the compound and was joined with the house behind the main pool," she says. Brenda bought her cottage two years ago and as far as she knows, it was built in 1985.

Before buying this cottage, she lived on Catherine Street for many years. She says about her current home, "It was in fair condition when I bought it. I just did cosmetic work, but it still took eight months. The gardens were here when I purchased it, but I redid the pool decks and planted a lot of the garden myself." Most of the citrus trees are freestanding in pots.

"I find this home to be very peaceful tucked back here." When she's not working, which is rarely, Brenda says she likes sitting on the porch, listening to the water feature and reading. While

Orchids are ubiquitous in Key West where they thrive.

she only paints for herself, she says, "It takes me out of my real estate head." Her little studio, reached from a hallway off the kitchen is filled

Clockwise from top left: The entrance to Brenda's cottage is discreetly hidden and very private. She enjoys gardening in pots so she can change and move them around at will.

The table is set for an impromptu lunch on the covered deck.

Blue and white is a favorite color scheme. Everyone loves a casual get together. No planning necessary. She gives total credit for the interior design to Michael Pelkey Designs: "He was instrumental in the way my home looks. He took me shopping for antiques and really worked hard getting the pieces to fit perfectly."

with all sorts of interesting retro collectibles from all over, "Some Michael found for me, the boxes on the wall came from Archeo (an unusual store in town) and belonged to a famous writer. I find the old black and white family photographs very comforting." There are favorite memorabilia all around the studio, like her dad's watch, his air force card, and other small tokens. While Brenda has excellent taste, she's a busy career woman and elicited help from Michael. Brenda is loyal to local artists and craftspeople. She has the work of Susan Sugar prominently displayed over the sofa in the living room, as well as in her office. Other local artists include Michael Palmer, Michael Klein, Mimi Hine, and Martha DePoo.

One wall of the bedroom was custom designed for maximum storage.

Wallpaper in bedroom from Beautiful Interiors.

Everything in this living room has a graceful softness around the edges. Nothing is too high contrast. Susan Sugar's painting fits right into this environment. Vase by Key West Pottery.

Clockwise from top left: The sweet little studio oozes charm and interesting objects abound.

The etched glass back door was repurposed and is perfectly suited to the retro vibe.

The back hallway leads out to the pool and deck.

A collection of old canisters fill a corner of the studio and are useful for storing lesser-used items.

Living on a Lane

Lanes are special places to live and the residents on lanes often create a mini community. Lanes crop up in the middle of main streets like Fleming or William. They might be marked or sometimes not. Sometimes there are just two or three houses on a ten-foot-wide lane, other times there might be half a dozen houses on a lane. When you discover a lane, you're sure it has been undiscovered until that very moment and each stroll down a lane is always a surprise.

Lanes have a way of luring you back again and again. A lane can look like an alley or even a driveway you've passed a hundred times. You're not sure if you're trespassing when you walk down some lanes. The houses on lanes are charming. Some are shotguns with no property at all. Others might have been enlarged and reconfigured with rather sprawling grounds, by Key West standards. I have never been down a lane that didn't make me want to return.

A House on Love Lane.

TREASURE BOX

Billy Foster loves living in a small space. He first came to Key West with friends in the 1990s and instantly knew this was the place he wanted to live. "It had the best vibe ever," he said. He returned many times, dreaming of living here. He was in the airline management business and stressed from the job. With a little savings, it didn't take him long to pack up and move to Key West. He has never looked back. "My first apartment," he says, "was on the second floor of a big Victorian house in Old Town. It was basically one room that opened onto a balcony that ran the width of the house. I loved it for four years, and then I needed more room. But not too much more! I was working different jobs, but mostly paying my rent by working at Kelly's Caribbean." Looking back Billy is reminded how hard people worked to be able to live here, and not much has changed.

Billy Foster lives in a crayon box bursting with colors. He admits to being a crazy person when it comes to color. He's lived in this little three-room, 500 square foot cottage for twelve years and has painted it many times. He says, "It's easy to paint small rooms and the colors don't overwhelm as they might in a larger space. I started with bright yellow, then olive green, then lime, then turquoise, and now kind of a blue teal." He's into his turquoise phase and the living room is a burst of enthusiasm. "I love the creaks in the floorboards and the texture of the Dade County

pine walls. They're original to the cottage." But most of all Billy appreciates the quiet on this hidden lane right in the middle of historic Old Town.

Billy Foster collects! It's his passion and he can't imagine ever being "done." His collections and interests change just as the interior of his cottage does. This is a work in progress. There's his grandfather's collection of fishing tackles and old tackle boxes, table fans, nautical prints, Mason jars, old clocks, mixing bowls, early typewriters, commercial signs, colorful thermos bottles, picnic carriers, and anything tropical. Everything in the cottage has been selected for a reason. It must resonate on some emotional or aesthetic level. "I am always looking for interesting things," he says.

The cottage is filled with carefully curated collections of retro objects and personal memorabilia from Billy's family, as well as Key West objects, and curbside finds. Aside from yard and estate sales, and the Salvation Army, this is one of the many ways folks in Key West recycle.

Billy says there's a Facebook page called "Curb Alert" that informs when someone is about to put something out on the curb for "first comers." Nothing lasts very long. While packed with interest, the cottage is always neat. Each arranged collection is a perfect artistic expression by itself and works as part of the entire dance. "Even though we have pretty much the same weather year-round, I change things by the seasons," he says. "I

Even before you come in the front door, the turquoise shutters, the curtained front porch, the rattan chairs beckon you to sit a while. The tropical palm trees that frame the property and provide privacy are quintessential Key West. You almost miss it, tucked so perfectly into the site.

The living room is where people love to linger.

The kitchen is open to the living room. Every square inch is designed to be eye-catching and, despite its size, Billy designed it to it function perfectly.

The bathroom is off the office and Billy designed the wall with paste-up palm leaves. The little retro medicine cabinet holds early bottles and the green theme is carried out with the glass medicine jars.

change the pillow covers, switch curtains out, add more or take away plants, and of course I go nuts at Christmastime." Billy loves mid-century ornaments and decorations and says his mom and sister, who live in Iowa, are always on the lookout for these items to send to him.

Since the cottage is super small, everything must have a dual purpose, especially where storage is concerned. When asked about his favorite items, he says he loves his grandfather's old fishing tackle and his great-grandfather's butterfly collection. Saving and taking care of things is definitely in Billy's DNA. "Both of these men took meticulous care of their possessions. We weren't wealthy so they took pride in what they collected and passed down," he explains. Billy says the best

compliment he gets is when people say, "It feels like home from the minute you walk in." He credits his mother for that. His father was in the army, so they moved often, sometimes to another country. She would still have the new house looking, feeling, and smelling great in a matter of hours.

When asked what advice he would give to people in his situation, he says, "Incorporating the things you've had forever into a new look every so often is a lot of fun. I think it works best when you have a lot of items that don't necessarily go together, to hang them all together. It will become very interesting, like a piece of art. The eye stops to view the curated items. If you sprinkle the collections everywhere it doesn't tell a story. It's confusing."

Billy Foster loves living in this small cottage on this stunningly beautiful island. And he can even ride his bike to work as a marketing director for a chain of hotels! "Life is good. This little cottage has seen a lot and protected many. I'm glad it's me for this chapter," he says.

Billy's bedroom is at the back of the house and opens onto a narrow deck filled with plants. The dramatic sign over the bed is a fun collectible. A bamboo fence and twinkling lights creates a magical, private space.

Billy calls this the Harry Potter room, where he carved out a little office space and arranged the items to look as if Ernest Hemingway might work here.

GUESTS ALWAYS WELCOME

Once you turn off the busy street and onto the lane it is suddenly quiet. And at the end of the lane, where there are only a handful of houses, sits this beautifully situated home—actually two houses joined by a central entryway. The house is a little imposing until the owners open the front door and graciously invite you in. You immediately feel relaxed, and the spaciousness of the room is unexpected.

One of the homeowners is an architect who designed the reconfiguration of the space, but purchasing a small piece of property in the back enabled them to expand the living room, add glass doors and look out onto a garden rather than a wall. This allowed for a little addition of a bedroom and bath, accessed up a few steps to the right of the living room.

When they are here the house is filled with guests. These two gentlemen are the epitome of what one thinks of as "southern gentlemen" even though they're from Cincinnati. They have hospitality down pat and the house responds beautifully to the easy, relaxed lifestyle that Key West is known for. If you arrived here "all wound up," you instantly let it go and that is the whole idea. The furnishings are tasteful, artistic, and stylish and designed for comfortable, slouchy living. This is not a house that fosters formality. You're encouraged to feel at home.

When we arrived, the homeowners had guests from Washington state and we assumed they were staying in the guest house (one of the two joined cottages). But this wasn't the case with

Inside the front door, this little open area, almost like an atrium, leads to the pool surrounded by lush plantings. It's hard to believe you're just seconds from a busy street.

these homeowners. Within minutes we understood the definition of gracious. "We live in the cottage," they said, "and leave the main house for our guests." But since the houses are connected it is easy to overlap socializing and go back to your home away from home when you need "alone" time. Everyone has privacy.

The front door is topped with a pediment repeated over the windows.

While they aren't large, there is a small private pool and hot tub that provide privacy for the homeowners and their guests.

The bedroom is awash in brilliant colors. The dramatic painted screen fills the wall in back of the bed.

The Dade County pine walls and stained-wood floors wrap the house in a warmth that contrasts with the cool black–and–white interior design.

A little eating area fits perfectly in one corner of the room. The back of the living room was expanded so there is a garden view that offers a feeling of open space.

The tranquil ambience is pervasive. Human sounds almost interfere with the quiet nature of the place and the garden might be the most important room in the house because everyone lives outdoors. The property is large by Key West standards, especially for a lane.

Key West brings out the child in most people who come here. You can have fun playing house. And for all the years these homeowners have been living here, they have never owned a car and always travel by foot or bicycle. It keeps them youthful. This is the beauty of Old Town. The Old Town Bakery is just a block in one direction and the Eaton Street Fish Market is a block in the other. Duval Street, where all the action takes place when it comes to restaurants and entertainment, is an easy sprint.

The front door is beautifully framed with a dramatic pediment and flanked by two lanterns. Everything about the property is crisp and neat and welcoming. While the house was completely transformed, the original footprint is the same.

Once inside a sort of atrium area, light pours in from the doors to the deck and the main pool. While one of the homeowners is an architect, he says when he's here they relax. "I've only done small jobs for friends," he says. Over time they have perfected the house to suit their needs and the comfort of their guests. They enjoy sharing their lifestyle with friends and family and what they created is a tranquil ambience that is pervasive.

The guest cottage, where the owners live, echoes the interior design and color scheme found in the main house, and is every bit as stunning.

A WORK IN PROGRESS

Hal Bromm and Doneley Meris have owned three houses in Key West since they came here in 1979. It was the town's historic character that appealed to them. Nothing was heavily renovated at that time. These were proud old houses that had survived countless hurricanes. Hal says, "We appreciated the variety of architectural styles that contributed to the unique sense of place, and reflected the island's past commercial activities. Most appealing were 'virgin' houses that were not restored, renovated, or altered, but simply maintained enough to leave their historic features intact." One of the houses they owned was right near their current house on the same lane. It had not been bastardized with insensitive renovations and alterations. Years later, they found the perfect house in the middle of that same lane across from the cemetery.

The day after they bought it, the house burned to the ground. Hal says, "Years after the fire I did a new design with an open floor plan. It was less wide than the original house, so a pool could go in between the two houses. Before the fire, the master plan was to have the pool where the pavilion is now located. It would have been only about forty feet long, running the width of the property." Today they have an unusual seventy-five-foot-long lap pool so that Hal, who is a swimmer, can do laps every day. "It is a dramatic black, reflecting pool, certainly unusual in Key West, and especially on a property in this location," Hal explained that seventy-five feet,

The bell lets the homeowners, who are probably busy in the garden, know that visitors have arrived. The sign states that this house was on the 54th Old Island Restoration Tour.

or twenty-five yards is a standard length for a lap pool, and it made sense to respect that. The design of such a large pool creates a great sense of spaciousness in an otherwise small property. Remember this is Old Town, on a narrow lane where houses are close enough to hear every

A discreet shell path lets you slip through to the gate that leads to the very deep property which includes the 75-foot pool.

This 75-foot pool is unusual on a lot this size in Old Town. Sculpture by Jim Raachi.

For many years Hal Bromm has been an art gallery owner in Tribeca, in Manhattan where he has exposed the work of many Key West artists. Doneley Meris is a grief therapist teaching at NYU and Columbia. He works primarily with the LGBTQ community. At the end of the day, Don unwinds with a bike ride around the island. The couple travel often, but spend much of their time in Key West where Hal has curated exhibitions for commercial and non-profit galleries.

While the garden is all-consuming and needs constant pruning and maintaining, their other passion is cooking for friends. Dinners at home, gathered around the big, glass conference table they "repurposed" keeps the creative world connected to other designers, writers and artists, all key players in the local arts, literary, and social scene. Don and Hal's intellectual passions have attracted a loose-knit, multi-generational "family" of sorts. They do a good job in recreating the spirit of Key West in its heyday when talented intellectuals gathered for entertainment and stimulating, joyful conversation. Hal and Don

cough and sneeze from your neighbors on both sides as well as the back.

You barely notice the house when you come down the lane. The little shell path is deliberately narrow, discreet, and almost hidden behind a hedge of tropical plantings. This is not an overly manicured property and in fact the homeowners find its maintenance an ongoing challenge. They are dedicated to and passionate about conservation and preservation, and are committed recyclers. They rarely miss a yard or estate sale, patiently sorting through the detritus of everyday life, looking for something useful to repurpose.

Michael Pelkey created a festive platter of fresh fruit with cheese and crackers and added a bunch of sunflowers to contribute to the lively atmosphere.

Drinks are served on the pavilion at the far end of the property, followed by a creatively prepared dinner on the deck poolside, and the conversation continues.

love it when their table is brimming. There is always an aura of good times in the air.

Several years ago, Hal was involved in an art project called Sculpture Key West, originally Art in the Park, started by sculptor Jim Raachi, who at the time was working as a ranger at Ft. Zachery Tailor State Park at the Truman Annex waterfront. Jim has several sculptures on this property. They're fun to come upon, as they aren't always obvious. They create subtle art that blends in with the environment, which fits the lifestyle of this couple quite well.

One of Jim Raachi's sculptures oversees the tropical drinks. There's always time to get together with friends in Key West. The weather is conducive to easy conversation late into the night. It's easy to forget it's winter.

A HOUSE WITH STYLE

A house that is unique, even on this island where uniqueness is expected, is a treat to experience. The owners of this house say, "We think interior design should speak to the environment where the house is located. It shouldn't look as though it could be anywhere." These homeowners came to Key West in 1996 to get away after the sudden passing of their dog, Archie. But it wasn't until 2002 that they bought this little cottage at the end of a lane. One of the homeowners, Don Bowie, is an author of three novels and a memoir, and they were attracted to the lively artistic community here. What appealed to them about the house was its Old Town location, off-street parking, and a pool. They didn't do any renovation. The biggest problem they had was finding appropriate furnishings for Key West. The kitchen table and chairs are circa 1948, Gilbert Rohde chairs, the settee, and the Handel "treasure island" floor lamp all came from Rago Auction the week they closed on the house. They say, "It was meant to be." Most of the accessories came from island shops.

The house is a study in authenticity. It is filled with antique wicker, Art Deco, "kitsch" and all things retro. Kitsch is a term applied to art and design that appeals to popular, rather than high art tastes. It is usually associated with nostalgic items from the past. This home is warm and inviting and looks lived in the way homey houses do. The antique Chinese and Iranian rugs were

The lamp, the bright red lampshade, a vase of shells, create a still life "tablescape" on the hallway table. Nothing here was put together haphazardly.

chosen for their Key West motifs in the weaves, for example, the Key deer and stylized chickens in two of them.

The homeowners, who also live in Manhattan, don't treat the house as precious and are confident enough to mix very expensive items

The front door is flanked by pots of tropical plants. Louvered doors adjust for light and air, but also provide privacy.

Looking down the hallway to the retro dinette set. Notice the overhead deco globe light.

The table is set with their "curbside" find of a complete set of plates that are perfect for this table. Doneley Meris's McCoy pots hold bunches of Easter colored flowers.

with those of lesser monetary value, but no less valuable for their interesting qualities. Good design always prevails.

Interesting collectibles seem to appear every-where, although the homeowners do not live on "a stage set." They are very much at home with their Key West lifestyle that they say is informal and unpretentious. The interior design exudes an air of playfulness, perhaps echoing the prevailing atmosphere associated with Key West.

Both homeowners cook elegantly casual meals, usually of local fish, and guests gather around the turquoise, steel-rimmed kitchen

table to share a meal. It all feels very comfortable and fun. "We prefer making dinner for just a few like-minded friends," they say. Most dinners are impromptu. Each room flows from kitchen to long living room and out to the deck where drinks are often enjoyed over lively conversation about the literary community and, of course, up-to-the-minute Key West gossip. No one is ever hurried. No one is ever bored.

The furniture is arranged to respond to easy conversation. One wall of the living room opens completely, so that this room is part of the out-doors. There is a built-in seating banquette that spans the living room and is perfect to accommodate seating for many. The exterior wall opens all the way so that the deck and pool become part of the house and seen from this vantage point. "The pool was here," they said, "We'd never seen a pool completely tiled like Chiclets!" Having lost a lot of the garden during Hurricane Wilma, they hired their neighbor, who had just started his landscaping business, to redo the surrounding gardens with native plants and trees. They are delighted with the results.

Serious artwork and collectibles mix with those of no particular provenance but are equally valued for their lightheartedness and contribution to the décor. It is not easy balancing whimsy and understated luxury and when you're in this space you're enticed to linger long after the sun goes down. When asked if the house is now finished, they say, "Never. It's still ongoing after twenty years."

The living room opens up so that the indoors and out become one room, doubling the living space.

A banquet seat fills one end of the living room facing the pool.

Right, top and bottom: Vintage postcards and retro souvenirs are treated with the same respect as more valuable art.

Facing page: The deck off the living room provides a space for drinks before dinner. The wrought iron table and chairs echo the turquoise of the kitchen table and chairs.

AN ARTIST'S RETREAT

If you were a romantic and had never been to Key West, but certainly read or heard about it, and were asked to describe a Key West home, based solely on imagination, you might conjure up "Turtle House." Two unassuming little cottages were built in the early 1900s to house Cubans brought here to work in the cigar factories. These 300 square foot, dilapidated dwellings fell into the right hands when, in 1976, architect Manfred Ibel (now deceased) purchased the first one, and ten years later, the second one with his wife, artist Susan Sugar. Connected by a covered deck, one contains a modest kitchen, bedroom, and living area, while the other is an open, light-filled studio where Susan spends as much time as possible. "I go back and forth to my apartment in New York City," she says. "I love the off-season in Key West the best, when many of the winter residents and tourists leave. It is peaceful and quiet, and I do my most creative work," she adds.

This home provides more than shelter for its owner. It is a Key West experience. There is an organic flow to life here, where daily living, making a meal, and making art are equally compelling. The layout of the structures interacts seamlessly with the property. Everything is in the right proportion and every room is connected to nature. This property is not trying to be something it isn't. There is a casual deliberateness to this enclave that takes a first-time visitor by surprise—in a very good way. It immediately has a calming effect as one is transported from the intrusions of the outside world. It is the personification of a simple, yet sophisticated lifestyle that few can achieve in a world that is moving very quickly. The owner doesn't know where the name "Turtle House" came from but it has come to mean an all encompassing home that is a safe

Two unassuming Conch cottages are joined by a deck. One is for living, the other for making art.

The front porch of the studio cottage is perfect for watching the lazy meanderings on this least-traveled lane.

A thatched roof covers the pergola that connects the two cottages. It's a wonderful place to work or enjoy an end-of-day drink with friends.

and cozy haven where the outside world temporarily disappears. Spending the day here reminds us to slow down and enjoy what we are doing. This property was designed to embrace and nurture a creative lifestyle. It is a mini retreat that nourishes the soul.

Susan points out that when Manfred Ibel first came to Key West he partnered with respected local architect Tom Pope, who has been responsible for many homes and renovation projects on this island. Manfred conceived of and built everything in this house. The materials are inexpensive and basic. Nothing is precious. This is an

honest dwelling and respected by its owner as well as friends who visit, and artists who come here for Susan's popular art workshops. From the moment you step onto the front deck you are transported to a Key West past that we are in jeopardy of losing. Susan is acutely aware of this and finds it reassuring to live this edited life where everything on this property and in these cottages has been deliberately curated. It takes determination to make sure everything is there for a purpose. Whether utilitarian or aesthetic, every object, every activity, every planting, must justify its existence.

The crocheted lace tablecloth, set under glass, was found on an island off of Venice.

Susan designed the louvered bathroom that can be accessed from the deck or studio. The weathered wood recedes into the environment and becomes part of the dwellings.

One of Susan Sugar's paintings on display outside the studio.

The rustic kitchen is small, compact, and extremely functional. It is easily accessed from the outside deck between structures.

The living area was an addition, with sliding glass doors that open to the deck, allowing the interior to have a relationship with the outdoors.

A small bedroom at the front of the "living" cottage.

A book of Susan's paintings lies open on the cabinet under one of her charcoal sketches of crossed Calla Lilies. The wooden "angel" sculpture is by local artist Duke Rude.

The glass wall of the studio slides open to allow easy access to the deck where Susan often unwinds with a friend or two at the end of the day. The pink and gold throw on the bench was found in Thailand and given to Susan as a gift from Manfred.

The original second cottage was gutted and completely custom built with unfinished plywood walls and surrounded by storage cabinets at the right height. Manfred planned it as an architectural studio, after which it became Susan's art studio where she holds her popular workshops. A loft and catwalk connect both sides of the room while leaving the ceiling open to the rafters.

Bahama Village

Located just southwest of Old Town, Bahama Village is a sixteen-block area off the beaten track. If you're into Florida Conch architecture, good eats, and an interesting history, it can all be found in Bahama Village. In the 1800s it was a settlement of Bahamian people of the Caribbean who settled in the area seeking stable income. While it has changed over the years, it has retained the flavor of its cultural past. The neighborhood boasts some of the best restaurants, including the iconic Blue Heaven. The building was once a home to Friday night boxing matches refereed by Ernest Hemingway. Bahama Village is an important part of what makes Key West so diverse.

An arched sign announces the entrance to Bahama Village off Duval Street.

ALL IN THE FAMILY

Carrie Disrud-Joris, her husband Tom Joris, and their three sons are the personification of the Key West spirit this family embraces. Their home is filled with unrestrained curiosity from a mélange of collectibles, art books, found objects, and art of their own creation, and that of their friends whose work they admire. This is the world they inhabit. They revere and celebrate the creative process. They share a visual vocabulary and enterprising spirit. The artistic conversation continues across two generations. Youthful exuberance might describe this family of five who create obsessively.

An artist's home isn't just a place to lay one's head down. It's also a workplace that often takes over all living space. It's a safe, private place to experiment. There is beauty in the artistic energy that feeds off itself in this home

A true artist's home is often idiosyncratic where art evolves. People are curious about artists' homes because they often reveal much about its inhabitants. The Disrud-Joris family is all about the art they create—some together, most individually. The family unit grew through their relationship with a desire to make art and they are surrounded by creative energy. They appreciate the beauty in the artistic chaos they live with—a mishmash of well-loved collectibles.

The house fits into the landscape, or rather, the landscape has emerged all around it, creating an oasis in the heart of Bahama Village. Houses are close together, but once you enter the gate by

An exotic air plant clings to a palm tree.

way of a long pathway from the street, you forget where you are. A cozy jewel might be an apt description of the little structure that the couple and their three sons call home. One of the sons, Andre Joris, a landscape designer, built a two-story tree house at the edge of the property where he resides. The pool he designed is discreetly set between the two structures.

Carrie and Tom bought their home in 1981 after coming for a visit from their home in Chicago. Carrie says, "The village gave us a sense of community and a breath of fresh air. The roads were still gravel and the chickens just set

The sign on the front gate announces this is an artist's home.

Looking through from the back through to the front of the house.

The living room/studio holds Carrie's recent creations. Her work is fanciful and fun and the embodiment of the Key West spirit.

Outdoor dining at its best.

the scene." Chickens still rule the roost in every neighborhood and folks here take them for granted, as just a different sort of resident.

The house needed tender loving care and so the couple began what would become a lifelong project, turning this home, built in 1906, into a place to ultimately raise their sons. Their oldest son, Andre, is a rare plant expert who began planting and using their garden as a canvas when he was eight years old. He never stopped, more than twenty years later. Rennie is the owner of Kalypso LLC studio and as an artist works on a variety of projects from restoration work to sculpting chairs. Dakota is in hospitality and loves traveling when not working at nearby Blue Heaven where the artwork on all the tables and walls is Carrie's. Dakota is also a water gardener.

"Tommie and I have been involved in the Key West art world since the early eighties. Tommie created the Bishops Knees sculpture at the southernmost point and I do murals for public places." Both Tom and Carrie are active in community affairs. Carrie describes the openness of the house as an inside/outside living space that was perfect for raising three boys. "The pool was literally the second thing we did, but the most important. With the dining table in the garden, pool parties have always been fun."

Carrie admits their house will never be finished. "Change is our middle name." The part the family loves most about the house is the outside/inside kitchen and dining room under the palm trees. This is a very lived in home. Carrie says, "It's organic by nature, so it's always changing to meet the challenges of many art projects we create in our living/art studio." Aside from her paintings, Carrie is a fabric artist who says about their tropical garden, "It's all Andre. All I do is love it."

The kitchen opens to the outdoors.

The garden exudes a variety of plantings that Andre designed around the pool.

LIVING WITH COLOR

Marge Holtz is a fabric artist who has been making art since she was a child and her parents sent her to the Columbus Gallery of Fine Art. She says, "I am an artist who paints and makes contemporary art quilts." Many of her quilts are in the collections of several major institutions and corporations. "Most of the work in our house is mine." Marge is an artist who loves color. She knows how to create art with color and how to decorate with color. Her house is exuberant and joyful. She has designed a one-of-a-kind space that incorporates vivid hues into every room to create the ultimate "wow" factor. Big doses of whimsy imbue this house with a common thread that keeps it all harmonious. The house exudes a sense of sophisticated playfulness.

Marge and her husband Rick came to Key West in the early 2000s and moved here permanently from Washington, D.C., in 2016. What attracted them was, aside from the weather, the bright colors, and the people. "The house was habitable," she says, "but very old and not in a charming way. The walls had been paneled with plastic stuff, but it was clean, the plumbing was working, and the neighbors were welcoming. Best of all there was enough room on the lot to put on an addition."

They knew they wanted three bedrooms, three baths, and a pool. They wanted lots of

The flower collage is by Elizabeth St. Hillair who Marge took a class from.

light and open space. Thinking like an artist, Marge says, "Think of it as a white canvas." With the restoration done, they now have a historic restoration star from the Historic Florida Keys Foundation. The house first appears on Sanborn

The painting above the purple door is by Marge Holtz, the homeowner.

The fabric on the poolside bench is one of Marge's quilts. You can see how tight this neighborhood is. You have to get along with your neighbors.

The living room is filled with colorful art, most by the homeowner.

Quilt art by Marge Holtz.

The dining table has one of Marge's table runners and the wall is filled with her art. Even the fabric on the chairs and the bowls are colorful.

fire insurance maps of Key West in 1884. The sawtooth addition that is now the living room appears on maps in 1912.

The overall design of the house is very modern and uncomplicated. It provides a good background for the quilt designs this artist creates for framing. They set the tone of the house. "We like to entertain," she says, "so large areas were important as well as easy access to the outdoor area." The deck roof is home to solar panels which help power the house.

A cheerful bedroom at the front of the house continues the colorful theme.

The couple's neighbor in Bahama Village, Andre Joris and his business partner designed and installed all the plantings and planned the garden with an emphasis on native plants. Marge says, "Though we love flowers, the iguanas love them too."

This retired federal employee, and naval officer as well as IT consultant, respectively, love to travel, principally outside of the United States. Rick is an avid volunteer with interests in history and carpentry. "He's my go-to guy for framing and mounting," Marge says.

Colorful fish adorn the poolside of the house.

Even the bathroom continues the colorful theme, started before you even enter the house.

A cigar box made into an instrument by the couple's son actually makes music.

Dog Beach next to Louie's Backyard, a favorite restaurant in the Casa Marina.

On the Edge of Town

There are many areas of the island where the houses are not as close as those in Old Town. Some say they're not as charming, but that's a matter of opinion. In a loose way, White Street and an extension of Von Phister create the dividing line between the Old Historic District and New Town. Once a commercial area with cigar manufacturing plants that employed as many as 600 workers in one factory alone, New Town is now more residential than commercial. In the 1800s the four-story Havana American Cigar Company was located on Third Street and many of the workers lived within walking distance of the factory. The houses in New Town, which is farther away from the town hub, are primarily built of concrete block rather than wood. Like those in Casa Marina they tend to have more property around them than those in Old Town.

The Casa Marina Hotel was built by the Flagler chain and opened on New Year's Eve, 1920. The streets that border the hotel are within easy access to the beach and town, forming an upscale neighborhood of houses built primarily in the 1950s. There are still many houses here that were built in the 1900s as well. The lots are larger than those in Old Town, and the houses in this area, known as Casa Marina, are perfectly suited to contemporary renovation.

A GROWN-UP TREE HOUSE

Matthew Talley, a business consultant, and his partner, Ricky Hamilton, a teacher, together with their son, Jerry Eller, moved to Key West just two months shy of Hurricane Irma in 2017 and began a two-year renovation project. The aerie they created, resembling a grown-up tree house, is where they would become part of this community. They said, "We loved taking advantage of the Key West lifestyle. Walking through town in the morning, working on the house and garden, relaxing poolside, and visiting our favorite restaurants and wine bars."

The story of how they came to Key West is a familiar one. It started in 2004, before Matt and Ricky met, when Matt visited his brother and family who were stationed in Key West. After they met, the couple began to vacation in Key West on a regular basis before finding what they thought would be a forever home.

"It was the only place on earth that we could relax and be ourselves," said Ricky. "We were able to enjoy the beauty of the water, the hospitality of the community, and, in general, island life." Soon after their son Jerry came along, they began to spend more time on the island, always making sure to be here for his birthday. "We loved having themed pirate parties for him and sharing his joy when shooting off a cannon on a real pirate ship."

When they first moved in, it was a very 1980s Art Deco–inspired home. "Jerry had his own red

mini refrigerator," Ricky says. There was red tile flooring throughout the living and kitchen areas. The bathrooms and kitchen were dated. The backyard was a mess. "Our goal was to introduce our own style while keeping the original charm of the house," Ricky continued.

However, they were inspired by the bungalow surfer vibe and named the house "Mahalo," meaning "Thank you" in Hawaiian. They started the project by defining what they knew they needed: a designated office for Matt, and room to grow as a family. They knew they wanted a relaxing porch to expand indoor/outdoor living. After living in the house for a while, they created their design ideas one room at a time.

Influenced by the Key West sunsets, the couple incorporated the oranges and blues into their renovations. They modernized the kitchen and used English white oak for the floor to emulate the color of sand. "This house was definitely meant for us," they said. It was serendipity because the right circumstances simply fell into place at the right time. They fell in love with the native lush vegetation around the property and, over the years, kept adding more.

Built in 1981, the original footprint was expanded and within two years after they bought it, this two-bedroom house was complete. "It was a labor of love," they said. "The biggest challenge was making the small square footage

A path leading to the backyard and pool.

The approach to the "tree house" is by way of a unique, curved stairway with mahogany tree trunk piers.

The office is just to the left inside the front door.

The massive front door opens into the office where the original Cuban tiles cover the floor.

The windows are repurposed from the Casa Marina hotel renovation. The open living room is filled with colorful fabric and artwork.

A row of orange stools outside the kitchen on the deck.

The kitchen space was redesigned to have an open flow by taking down walls and peninsula and ceiling to expose the high beams. The orange Smeg stove and hood influenced the colorful accents throughout the house. They extended countertops and cabinets and added a full pantry.

seem spacious and functional for year-round, family living. We opened the kitchen to flow into the house by taking down walls and opening the ceiling to high beams." They extended counter-tops and installed high-end appliances. They are quick to point out the importance of indoor/out-door living. When asked what one word explains how they feel about the house, the answer was, "Comfort."

Shortly after we photographed the house Matt and Ricky were faced with a big decision. Their son, Jerry, had educational needs that were not being met by the local school. With a big family support system in Washington, D.C., this family decided it would be best to leave Key West so that Jerry would be surrounded by cousins and grandparents and have the education they felt he deserved. I'm sure their next project will be equally wonderful, creative, and exciting and the community looks forward to welcoming them back in the future. Everyone who's had a taste of Key West always returns.

The "Nana Suite" (aka guest room) has the perfect tropical vibe from the wall and furniture colors as well as the fun accessories like the Flamingo lamp. The sky window provides views of swaying palms as well as sunrises and sunsets. Ricky says, "It's like living in a Pam Hobbs painting."

A pathway through the tropical gardens leads around to the backyard and pool.

The back of the house is surrounded by tropical gardens, designed by locally based ZenScapes, for complete privacy in this densely populated neighborhood.

The family wanted the yard to be English garden meets tropical vegetation. The space, once renovated, was used all the time for watching television, reading, and barbecuing. It became the quintessential indoor–outdoor living room.

Inspired by vintage Hawaiian estates, the back porch colors emulate the ocean.
Overlooking the pool below, the newly created porch extends the living area. A chandelier,
typically found in unexpected places, lends a touch of romance in Key West homes.

LIVING WITH ART

What could be more convenient for an artist than to have a home next door, or rather part of the property where you have an art gallery? Life doesn't get better than that. Helen Harrison is an artist who paints and makes exquisitely elegant sculpture. Her gallery, Harrison Gallery, features Helen's work as well as that of artists doing cutting edge work in all sorts of media. It's always a surprise to go to a Thursday night "Walk On White" opening, if only to discover what is au courant. It seems Helen always finds the most interesting artists to showcase. I met Helen and her musician husband Ben many years ago and have been a fan of both their work ever since. Their life is organically entwined with their family, their art, and the community of Key West.

Helen and Ben arrived in Key West in 1979 when they sailed their boat, *La Dulce Mujer Pintada* (*The Sweet Painted Lady*), into the Key West harbor. Ben says, "We arrived in a roundabout way from Costa Rica, where we had built the boat and lived aboard for eleven years." He wrote a book, *Sailing Down the Mountain*, about that experience, and I was privileged to write the review for the *Key West Citizen*.

As far as what attracted the couple to their house and gallery, Ben says they needed a shop first and foremost when they arrived on the island. While living aboard their sailboat, he and Helen rented studio space at Truman Annex and they wanted to find something similar. Their first

The coral steps and runner on the white painted floor is so cheerful. The paintings are by Melinda K. Hall and the mirror is by Jimmy Wray.

son was five and they needed space for bicycles and such, much more room than a sailboat allowed. "In 1986 we bought the gallery and house next door and started fixing it up." Ben says, "It is the one and only house we've ever owned and where we raised our two children."

The entrance to the house is an extension of the gallery. Paintings and sculpture seem to wind up in one space or the other, depending on the current show. The stone sculpture "Wind God" is by Matthew Lineberger and made of Key West marl stone.

The turquoise steps provide a straight path between the kitchen and the studio/gallery.

When choosing artists to represent, "Craftsmanship with unique qualities and originality speak to me," she states. "I lean toward objects and sculpture."

Helen and Ben have no trouble putting their skills learned from boatbuilding to work when it comes to the house. Last year they laid a new solid oak floor in the kitchen. Helen says, "The simplicity, along with the historical significance of the house being over a hundred years old, make it an intriguing part of our everyday lives."

As for their community involvement, Helen and Ben are members of the Studios of Key West and last year they were honored to receive the

The kitchen looks directly into the studio that leads to the gallery. The large painting is by Beth Nablo.

After the boat, the house seemed enormous. They laughed about not using the living room for the first year or so after adjusting to land. And the renovations took at least that long. "We were the 'skilled labor' and our décor was chaos," they said. When living on the boat, storage space was scarce, so Helen is used to staying away from clutter. She likes things neat and, to this day, is selective about her surroundings.

The house is their private extension of the gallery where Helen shows her work. "I really enjoy living with my artist friends' work," she says. It offers inspiration and provides special memories.

Golden Mango Award, given annually by TSKW for individuals contributing to the arts community. Their son, Cole, an underwater photographer, is following in his parents' artistic footsteps, at the moment photographing exotic fish in Fiji. His large-scale underwater prints are featured in the gallery.

Just like Ben and Helen, I have my favorite spots to perch in their house. I love sitting in their kitchen and looking straight out into the gallery courtyard, or in the other direction into their garden. Both views involve art. Helen says, "From my kitchen I see into the studio that leads to the gallery. This is my most traveled path." The gallery is Helen's door to the world, and she finds

Here is where Ben writes songs that keep the local culture of Key West alive.

The kitchen is filled with art.

it interesting to see who rings the bell to come into the gallery. Helen has an uncanny memory for names and faces, especially those who have been clients of the gallery. "Collectors always turn into friends," she says. I own a Helen Harrison creation and it's one of my favorite possessions. It is timeless.

On the other hand, Ben, as a songwriter/ musician, remembers lyrics and he still owns his first guitar. Ben sings of characters that long-time locals recognize, and everyone loves to hear about. His live concerts are always anticipated and are a sellout.

One of Helen's sculptures, The Queen, is mixed media made from Palm fiber that gleams with 24-carat gold that resides majestically in the garden.

The avocado green leather sofa is the perfect vantage point for a private concert of Ben's music. The wood sculpture of The Haitian Woman was carved by Mark Volcy. Helen's sculpture on table to right. Large painting by Beth Nablo.

The gallery is where magic happens. The pears, coconut made of bronze and titled "Coco Blanco," and palm fiber sculpture are by Helen Harrison. The framed photographs are by Charlie Gaynor.

The area between the main gallery and the outside back studio/gallery is the office. Helen also uses this space as an intimate work environment. It is as interesting to see the work in progress as the finished product.

The Meadows

The little square area bordered by Newton Street, Truman Avenue, Eisenhower Drive, and White Street is a special part of the island known as the Meadows. This lovely quiet, historic neighborhood just off to the side of Old Town was once farmland. Key limes, vegetables, and dates were cultivated for island residents and for commercial enterprises. Chickens and cattle were raised on this part of the island before it was developed for residential use. Today wood houses, representing a variety of architectural styles, fill this family neighborhood. Homeowners here for the most part know each other and there is a feeling of warm comradery like you find in many small-town neighborhoods. It is a community within a community.

This eyebrow house in the Meadows looks quite grand and imposing, but the interior is actually warm and cozy.

LIVING IN AN EYEBROW

An unusual type of revival-style residence in Key West is charmingly referred to as an Eyebrow house. While there are thirty examples of such houses in Key West, they do not exist anywhere else in Florida. The roof eaves extend well beyond the top of the facade, shading the upper story of the house. The low roof line also serves to catch cool breezes and deliver them to the rooms inside. The "eye" windows on the second story are smaller than those on the first floor, but are partially hidden behind the overhanging roof "brow." While only a view of the front porch is provided from these windows, the rooms receive plenty of indirect sunlight during the day.

Mitzi Krabill and Bonnie Jones first came to Key West to visit family around 1981. What made them stay were the usual attributes, weather primarily. But they also like getting out on the water, the simplicity of living here, the gay and lesbian acceptance, and easy bike rides to everything. "We liked Shorty's Diner, Fast Buck Freddie's, the Sands Beach where The Reach is now, La Te Da tea dances and Atlantic Shores Tea Dance, and the $2.00 Sunday dinners at the Monster."

The eyebrow house they bought in the Meadows in 1995, was built in 1892, but before this house, they owned a duplex on Virginia Street where they rented out the upstairs apartment. They did extensive work to this house, most importantly removing interior paneling, which revealed the original Dade County pine walls. They removed a wall between the living and dining rooms to create a better flow to the kitchen, and much more work including the addition of a sizeable pool. After the initial renovation they won the coveted Historic Florida Keys Award.

Mitzi Krabill has been a Key West real estate broker for many years and Bonnie, now retired, was a FedEx courier. They are considered fixtures in this community. Bonnie says, "We're lucky that we like the same style, old and cozy. We knew

The porch is where these homeowners spend most of their time.

The French doors were part of the renovation in the dining room, allowing a feeling of being outdoors.

The living room at the front of the house is filled with the couple's favorite things, including the model pond boat between the front windows. Michael Pelkey and Laura Barletta helped Mitzi and Bonnie with the furnishings when needed.

we wanted to live in a real conch house, especially an eyebrow, and this one had a good feel to it. It had good bones." Mitzi grew up in Ohio, but moved to Boston after college where they both became teachers. They met in 1974. Bonnie comes from Marblehead, Massachusetts, and this house reminded them of a Saltbox house in New England. As a real estate agent, Mitzi knew the island well and they both were attracted the Meadows.

They love the comfort of this warm and inviting home. To play against the houses symmetry, and complement its original details, they

The main bedroom is on the first floor and the pine walls are original to the house. These eyebrows tend to be more spacious, with higher ceilings than the cottages in Old Town. The painting of their house with their antique truck in the front has a prominent place over the bed.

layered furnishings, filling the house with local art, antiques, and their favorite objects. They've created an elegant combination of old and new for an intimate year-round home. When asked which of the rooms they like being in the most, Mitzi likes the kitchen with the exposed pine walls and cabinets and the fact that it opens onto the back deck and pool. Bonnie likes the back porch, which is their winter living room and says, "It's a good place to take a nap or watch a football game on TV."

The kitchen cabinets are made of Dade County pine and this room flows into the "winter living room" and has easy access for serving drinks poolside. A Sangria party is about to happen. Bonnie and Mitzi bought bunches of sunflowers from a market stand on their way home from a trip up the Keys.

A SANCTUARY FOR ONE

Elizabeth Chamberlain's home embodies all that's wonderful about living in a tropical paradise. Her house in the Meadows proves that sophistication and fun aren't mutually exclusive.

As an artist she knows how to create a strong impact that makes a room memorable. This also describes her personality.

Elizabeth purchased this little Conch cottage in 2014. It was the epitome of what the real estate brokers call a "fixer upper." But Elizabeth earns her living as a real estate broker and had no trouble seeing this as a good opportunity. She instinctively knew she was up for turning this wreck into a little jewel box. This dynamo of a homeowner, flying through town on her bicycle, is a force to be reckoned with. She knows how to make things happen.

Elizabeth Chamberlain is not only a successful real estate broker with a roster of loyal clients who somehow always become her friends, but she is also an accomplished artist who, when not

The front bedroom was designed as an art studio where the homeowner's two springer spaniels have beds for watching their owner at work.

This stylish house in the Meadows was once "a wreck" before artist Elizabeth Chamberlain bought it in 2014.

showing houses, can be seen almost anywhere on the island creating her plein air paintings that are gobbled up by onlookers even before the paint is dry.

When she found this rundown shotgun cottage, she knew she could turn it into an ideal home for herself and her two springer spaniels, Jude (a rescue) and Pearl. "They're my audience," she says. When we arrived to photograph the house it was clear that the dogs felt they owned the place and their master was simply there to do their bidding.

Shotgun houses are common in Old Town, but rarer elsewhere on the island. This style of house has a hallway that runs from the front door to the living room at the back, thus its name. Most Key West homes have the bedrooms located in the front so that all the living areas can open to the back of the property. What might have become a guest room in the front, just off the front hallway, was claimed as a studio, although Elizabeth tends to like working in the open air and carved out a little studio overlooking her new mini pool—just right for one person to cool off. This home suits her to a T and is her refuge, and where she gets inspired. Her bedroom and private bath (there's a powder room off the hallway between the bedrooms) are soft and feminine and as attractive as the rest of the house

The homeowner's soft soothing bedroom is enlivened with one of her paintings.

This ultra-modern bathroom is tucked neatly off Elizabeth's bedroom.

A narrow refrigerator fits neatly into this efficient, streamlined kitchen.

Bowls of green and white fruits and veggies and Elizabeth's paintings provide colorful accents.

The living room is sophisticated and sleek. The wonderful leopard fabric chairs swivel and are chic and super comfortable. When the room is small it's wise to choose each piece of furniture for maximum impact.

The living room spans the width of the back of the house. The furnishings are unpretentious and offhandedly chic. A streamlined, incredibly functional, up-to-the-minute kitchen is open to the living room and the deck. This is where this homeowner works, has casual meals with friends, and feels most comfortable. It's her sanctuary at the end of the day.

Elizabeth's outdoor painting studio is ideal when she doesn't want to work inside.

No color scheme is as endlessly versatile as white and leafy green. It is at once crisp and contemporary, romantic and exotic as well as dramatic. You could decorate a whole house with it and still make every room completely different. Few color schemes in a tropical setting are quite so pleasing on so many levels. And it's easy to introduce a third color, igniting the exotic with hot pink, yellow, or cantaloupe orange. Elizabeth does all this with her own paintings, adding color accents, texture, and patterns to the walls.

A work in progress.

Acknowledgments

Whenever I am working on a magazine article or a book, I am always asked, "How do you find the houses to photograph?" It's a good question. I start with one or two recommendations from someone whose opinion I trust. In this case I relied on my friend Michael Pelkey, whose innate good taste and the respect he has earned in Key West as an interior designer were invaluable. I have been in Key West for over thirty-two years and have been in some terrific houses that I was grateful to be able to include as well. And then one house leads to another, and I find my inbox full of suggestions for "a house you must see." Specifically, I was interested in mostly small Conch cottages that have been creatively renovated and decorated with respect for the history of the house and where it fits into the fabric of the island. I always interview homeowners so that I can tell in their words what they saw in the house that spoke to them, what they did to enhance it and why, and to tell their story in an informative and interesting way. I always say, "Your home tells the story of who you are." The homeowners are part of the Key West community and how they interact with the island and what they do here is as interesting as what they did to improve their homes.

I am incredibly grateful for Michael's good taste and intuitive instinct. He styled the rooms with respect for the homeowners and in a way that enhanced how they live and enjoy sharing their homes. The chosen houses were just a handful of those we could have included, had there been more room. It was my intent to present a variety of styles so that you, the reader, would get as broad a view as possible of Key West style and maybe come away with some ideas to incorporate into your own homes wherever you live. The gardens too were as important as the houses and I'm indebted to those experts who offered advice on tropical gardening. The following homeowners and extraordinary experts in their fields made this book possible. I am indebted to them for opening their doors to me, Michael, and Tamara for her exquisite photographs, without hesitation and to the experts who offered advice. They are: Laura Barletta, William Marraccini, Kate Hoffman-Brown, Don Desrosiers, Will Dewey, Fran Decker, Kenny Weschler (gardener), Terje Stenstad, Ralph Firestone, Gary Merriman, Jill Gudoian, Henrik Holbaek, Claus Jensen, Craig Reynolds (landscape architect), Gregory Long, Scot Newman, Brenda Donnelly, Billy Foster, Hal Bromm, Doneley Meris, Carrie Disrud-Joris, Tom Joris, Harvey Klinger, Don Bowie, Marge and Rick Holtz, Matt Talley, Ricky Hamilton, Jerry Eller, Helen Harrison, Ben Harrison, Mitzi Krabill, Bonnie Jones, Jim Raachi, Susan Sugar, Don Beck, Larry Eynon, Elizabeth Young, head of the Arts Council, Dawn Wilkins, Christine Scarsella of Art@830, and Ron of Harpoon Harry's.

I am extremely grateful for having Lauren Younker as my editor at Pineapple Press, for her patience, understanding, and consummate professionalism; production editor Jessica Thwaite, for her unending patience; and Kaska Kwiecien for coming to my rescue with the editing of photographs and for her computer skills. There aren't enough ways to thank my agent and friend of more than twenty years. Linda Konner has always worked tirelessly on my behalf, going the extra mile when representing my best interests. I am a better writer because of her diligence and patience. And to all the folks of Key West who read my column in the *Key West Citizen* each week and who let me know when a subject is of particular interest. I am grateful to be part of this very accepting community.

—Leslie Linsley

About the Author

Leslie Linsley is one of this country's best-known authors of crafts, decorating, and home-style books, which include over seventy titles. While in college majoring in journalism, Leslie sold her first book, *Decoupage: A New Look at an Old Craft* (Doubleday). It led to a long and successful career in publishing. For many years Linsley, with her graphic-designer husband Jon Aron, packaged and produced dozens of how-to craft books for major publishers. With the publication of *Nantucket Style* in 1990, she then moved into writing books on architecture and interior design with a focus on lifestyle about how people decorate, renovate, restore, and live in their homes.

Aside from books about Nantucket and Key West, Florida, she has partnered with *Country Living Magazine* for several publications. Linsley divides her time between Nantucket Island (where she has lived most of her life) and Key West and writes a weekly newspaper column, "At Home in Key West" for the *Key West Citizen*, and contributes to many national magazines. Leslie has been a guest on *Good Morning America*,

Jon Aron

The Today Show, and *Oprah* as well as numerous appearances on HGTV programs. For fifteen years Linsley was the contributing craft editor for *Family Circle Magazine*.

Sunset is always cause for celebration in Key West.